POOR ME TO SOUL RICH

Spiritual Currency for the Mind, Heart & Soul

Anthony D Brice

Dedicated to my granny, Edna M Jones. Thank you for all the sacrifices you made so that I can have a dream. Thank you for praying for me when I didn't know how to pray for myself. Thank you for teaching me the meaning of family. You told me that everyone needs help sometimes and that if I can help someone, I should. You reminded me that one day I can be in the same position and I would want someone to do the same for me.

I hope I made you proud.

CONTENTS

POOR ME TO SOUL RICH

INTRODUCTION

It was April 1, 2006, and I was headed to the first day of my new job in a new city. After long consideration, I gave up my old life in an attempt to start over and create something better. I was a young man, three years removed from college, engaged to be married, and life was catching up with me faster than I could have ever imagined. My fiancé was a month away from graduating from college, and we decided that this move marked a fresh start for us.

Little did I know, within a month of my first day at the new job, the world that I knew would come crashing down. My fiancé and I broke up, and she was no longer moving to be with me after graduation. I was forced to move back home to the very streets I felt I worked so hard to escape.

I had a clear vision for what my life was supposed to look like and how it was supposed to go. I planned everything down to the letter. On that day, it felt as if those plans went up in flames, and all I was left with was the ashes of those faded memories. It's one thing to know that these difficult experiences are a part of life, but it's a totally different thing to be the person going through it.

Coming from where I'm from and seeing the things that I've seen, I used to feel like I started from the bottom, and at this time, I felt like life pushed me right back down to the bottom. The thing that gave me the most hope was that I came from a fearless, loving, and praying grandmother. She was an amazing woman who loved God, and she did everything in her power to make sure that I did, too.

Life ironically brought me back to the home where she helped raise me, where I established my foundation of Faith. I had built my life on that foundation, and that strengthened me to not only endure but to achieve. As difficult as things were, at no point did I not think that things would work out. I just didn't know when or how.

The bedroom I was sleeping in was the same room that my mother, my little brother, and I used to share growing up in my grandmother's house. Talk about a humbling experience, as if I needed one.

One day, I remember receiving a package addressed to me from an unknown source. I hadn't ordered anything, and it didn't say where it came from. At the time, very few people even knew I moved back. The package contained a DVD for a movie that I never heard of. With all the mystery surrounding this surprise package, it made me more intrigued to see what this movie was about. It was about so much more than I could have imagined...

The movie itself was simple in concept but profound in the message. The movie was created by a woman who, during the lowest point in her life, felt that she received a great revelation about how to transform your life and create the experiences of your dreams. It featured a number of different thought leaders and experts who talked about the hidden power that all humans possess to use our minds to create our own reality. The movie showed people who claimed to have used their minds to heal themselves, become successful, and find love using the law of attraction. The movie itself went on to be a huge success and sparked a massive movement in the personal growth industry. The movie was called The Secret.

To say the least, it was an exciting message for me to receive at that time, and any time I hear something that I think can help others, I am compelled to share it. I called one of my close friends, Mark, and told him about this great movie and that I had no idea where it came from. He was excited to hear about it and laughed to himself as he revealed that, in fact, he was the person who sent it to me.

That moment marked the beginning of a life-changing journey of self-exploration. I dedicated the next 12+ years of my life to deeper study into personal power, personal growth, the law of attraction, spirituality, psychology, and anything that could positively impact the human condition.

READY...SET...CHANGE THE WORLD

I learned about all of these great things that were helping me to look at different aspects of life in a totally different way. The insight and principles that I was learning about were more than any of the formal education that I ever received combined. I remember thinking to myself, why is none of this taught in schools!? Surely, teaching kids about self-love, success principles, and mindset are crucial to their development into becoming the best versions of themselves they can be.

I told myself that if schools weren't going to teach it, it was my responsibility to at least share some things that I knew could make difference. I felt like if people just got a small portion of it, it could be life-changing. I would talk about dreaming big, creating a successful life, and having amazing relationships. Helping people understand these principles was going to change lives...so I thought.

First, I set up a blog, and I was going to post these profound messages that people wouldn't be able to get enough of. After a year of very little traffic and engagement, that idea crashed and burned.

Then, social media was really taking off, and everyone was on Facebook. I thought that would be the perfect place to reach the people I thought could benefit from this information. Though I was able to reach a larger and more engaged audience, the things that they were most engaged with had nothing to do with my core message of personal power and self-empowerment. I wasn't talking about any drama, any negativity, anything funny. I wasn't fighting, and I wasn't an aspiring model. I only mention those because, at the time, they were apparently the most popular content (still may be).

It would take an entire book to list all of the outlets I chose to try to get my message out, including several blogs, guest writing on websites, several Facebook business pages, Twitter, Pinterest, Tumblr, and several others that I don't remember. With each failed attempt, I began to get frustrated because even though I knew the value of what I was putting out, others didn't see it. In hindsight, I understand that it isn't anyone's fault, and I can't blame anyone for not seeing what I see, even if I feel like it can help them. I ended up stepping away from it all for a while to determine if I should just be more concerned with what was going on in my personal life instead of being so consumed with getting this message out.

HERE COMES INSTAGRAM

It seemed that the less of a fan of social media I became, the more it became a must-have for any brand or business who wanted to reach the masses that were flocking to it by the millions a day. By the time I found Instagram, it was already becoming the preferred social media outlet for many millennials. I never planned on using it much, and I rarely posted pictures.

After years of being on there, I noticed that some people were using the platform to spread positive messages and quotes. I still didn't post much, but as time went on, I noticed that the quotes received more likes and feedback than my regular pictures did. I didn't know whether to be offended or to take it as a promising sign that positive information and perspective was gaining popularity.

I NEEDED THIS

The crazy thing is, while I was trying to use my experiences to teach others, they were teaching me so much about myself. I was reminded that purpose has nothing to do with other people accepting or listening. My purpose has everything to do with my obedience to my God-given vision and gifts. It was never my job to understand the message; my only job was to speak my truth, no matter how many people were listening. So, that's what I did.

I began to receive comments and messages from people all over the world about how they were impacted by my messages. There was one comment that I kept seeing, which inspired the writing of this book. There was one resonating quote that was coming from people of all ages, backgrounds, race, religion, and geographic locations. The one comment that people leave most on my posts and message me is, I Needed This!

I would get messages from people pouring their hearts out about how much they are going through or how much my post inspired them. They would send messages about how much they needed to hear that exact message at that exact moment. Many people expressed that they felt the message was just for them.

The revelation is that no matter what it looks like on the outside, people are dealing with real life behind those pictures and posts. People are hurting and don't know how to deal with it. People are in pain and don't know how to heal. So many people are sick and tired of being sick and tired that they don't even know who they are anymore. People are just existing with a feeling of diminished value and no sense of self.

People are bombarded with quotes that sound good, but they lack the context and understanding to even know how to apply them to their lives, especially when they are in the middle of their trials and tribulations. There is a generation of dreamers who are doing everything they were told to do to be successful, and they are still struggling. There are so many of us with the capacity to be great, but it gets harder and harder to see the greatness through all of that bad.

There's no better way to say it than to plainly say that *people are going through it*!

This book isn't about me claiming to have all of the answers or to say that my life is some perfect fairytale of happiness, success, and fulfillment. Nope! I've dealt with hardships, and I am going through it right along with you. I may not know everything, but I know this: no matter how things may appear, everyone is struggling with something. EVERYONE!

This book isn't about talking to people; it's about speaking into people. Foregoing all the basic, redundant quotes about *thinking positive* or *you can do anything you put your mind to*. This book penetrates through all of the masks, the pretending, the fakeness, and the all the lies we may tell ourselves, and speaks directly to the soul. The soul will always be the source of your true self. You can play happy on the outside, but if the soul isn't fulfilled, you will know. You can try to ignore it, but deep down, you can feel it.

Our lives are so much about the journey of our souls experiencing this life in the physical and in the spiritual at the same time. The soul is always searching for meaning from all its experiences. It searches for the meaning of life, of purpose, and of love and tries to determine how to process all of those dynamics simultaneously in an attempt to live a happy and fulfilling life.

At the end of the day, we all just want to understand our purpose and truly know who we are as a person. We all ideally want the same things from our lives. We want to be happiest versions of ourselves. We want to give and to receive the fullness of love. We want to feel fulfilled in our body, in our minds, in our hearts, and in our souls. We want our lives to have meaning.

HOW TO GET THE MOST OUT OF THIS BOOK

Poor Me to Soul Rich contains over 200 reflections about some of the deepest aspects of life that have the most impact on who we are, who we become, how we feel, and what we can accomplish. These aspects include self-love, your life of success, love and relationships, friendships, spirituality, and much more.

Some of the entries are shorter, and some are longer, but if you really pay attention, they all contain valuable insight. The passages aren't meant to just be read, they are meant to be felt. Take your time to really try to understand what's being said. How does it make you feel? Does it give you a different perspective? What does it make you think about?

Take your time with it. After you read one passage, meditate on it for a while and see what revelations it introduces to your mind and to your spirit. Even when you come back and read the same passage at a different time, more than likely, you will see something that you didn't see the first time or feel something that you didn't feel before.

Even though I think that this book can feed our hungry souls for today, the words and the principles are timeless. You can pick it back up in a year and receive new revelations and perspective that can have a big impact on your life. As you grow, the book will subconsciously grow with you because you will always be changing.

You may not currently relate to all of the passages, but I guarantee you will read several pieces that speak to you. Some will speak to your thoughts. Some will speak to your feelings. Some will speak to your heart. No matter which part of you it speaks to at the time, it's going to be up to you to listen and be obedient to your vision.

I want to thank you from the very bottom of my heart for taking the time to read this collection of my work. This is a dream come true and the culmination of years of searching within myself. This was inspired by the experiences and insights of all who have shared their testimony and their energy with me. I hope that through this powerful collection of shared energy that at least one life is impacted and that it sparks a revolution of souls with a mission to empower others.

Thank you for investing in yourself. There is no doubt in my mind that it is the best investment that we can make. I believe that this investment not only benefits you and your life, but it also impacts the people you love and those around you. All energy is contagious, and by infusing yourself with positive energy, you infect all those around you.

Proverbs 4:7 of the Bible (NKJV) says:

Wisdom is the principal thing; Therefore get wisdom. And in all of your getting, get understanding.

I hope that this book helps you gain a deeper level of clarity into yourself, your life, and all that comes with it so that you can enrich your soul. May you recognize your divinity and your power to create the life that is meant for you.

POOR ME TO SOUL RICH

Spiritual Currency for the Mind, Heart & Soul

IT'S YOURS

When you look at your life, and it doesn't reflect what you want, but you still keep believing. You will not be defined by your past. Your current circumstances are not your reality. The vision that you see in your mind and the dream that you hold in your heart is your reality. Every time you close your eyes, you can see it, you can feel it, and you can taste it. Your spirit has claimed it. No matter how hard it gets, no matter how many bad days you have, and no matter how many times you want to give up, something in you keeps holding on. Every time you question if it can really even happen, it keeps coming back. That is the difference between those who succeed and those who fail. Those who live the life they want and those who live the life they can. Those who listen to their spirit and those who listen to the world. What's for you, is *for you*, but you have to know it beyond a shadow of a doubt. Today. Right now. At this very moment. It's yours!

YOUR DREAMS WILL BE TESTED FOR AUTHENTICITY

Your dreams will be tested. I don't care who you are, there is no way around it. All dreams are tested for authenticity. What does that mean? If you really want what you say you want, life is going to test you. If you quit after things don't work out the first few times, then you really didn't want it that bad. If someone can talk you out of your dream or make you feel like you don't have what it takes, then you definitely didn't want it in the first place. Life will not only prove to you what you really want, life will make you prove to yourself who you really are. I believe that the purpose of these tests are not to make you quit, but to grow you into the person you need to become to fulfill this dream. It's going to take a certain kind of person to get there, but more importantly, it's going to take a certain kind of person to stay there. Being successful is one thing. Staying successful is another thing. So, remember why you're doing it and know that you are not being broken down. Rather, you're being built up. Knowing that these tests will be coming better prepares you for the journey ahead. You won't be prepared for everything that happens, but you know that how you respond to those things is what will make or break your success.

If you really want it as much as you say you do, then you won't allow anything to stop you from moving forward. No matter how many times you may get knocked down, you will stand back up every time. Don't worry about proving it to them - prove it to yourself.

CHOOSE YOU

S ometimes, doing what we feel is best for us means leaving some people behind. That can cause us to feel guilty about bettering ourselves and our situation although someone else is choosing not to. We have to understand that it's okay to choose ourselves when it comes to growing and doing what's best for us. In no way should you feel that you're not being loyal by choosing not to follow the path of a loved one. A true friend will understand, support, and respect your decision. *Choose you!* Not in a selfish way, but in a way that empowers you to change your life for the better.

HAPPINESS ISN'T

Happiness isn't a destination. It is a combination of a state of being and a state of becoming. It is a life-long journey filled with lessons, mistakes, and revelations. This is so important to understand so that when life gets hard, you are better prepared to navigate the obstacles and come out of it stronger than before.

DON'T BLOCK YOUR BLESSINGS

To allow the things we want to come into our lives, we have to put ourselves in a position to receive them. It's possible to want our circumstances to change but blocking our blessing by not following our life's vision and taking action on it. You know what kind of life you want. You want happiness, you want stability, you want love, and you want peace of mind. It's not always a matter of wanting it – sometimes, it's a matter of living it. You put yourself in position to receive by having a crystal-clear vision of what you want, believing that it's already yours, and taking action on those beliefs. Every day, you have to think about it, you have to speak it, you have to feel it, and you have to do it. Put yourself on the same level of vibration as your vision, and eventually, it will become a reality.

FAILURE DOESN'T MEAN FAILED

Failure may be the most important part of becoming successful at anything. Failure teaches you the most valuable lessons in getting to your destination and creating the quality of life you want. Go research anyone who has ever accomplished anything great, and you will find that their path to greatness started with a failure. There is a huge difference between failure and failed. You only fail when you quit. As long as you keep working toward what you want, success is inevitable. I'm not saying it's going to be easy, but I am saying it's necessary. No one's success is spared from failing, and you will not be either. You will fall, and you will fail (a lot). It is a part of the process, so accept it as a part of your journey to your destination. So, what are you going to do with your failures? Make excuses, give up, feel sorry for yourself? OR, are you going to dust yourself off, use what you've learned, make adjustments, and get things on the course to your goal? The choice is yours...

GET YOUR MOUTH RIGHT

Be careful with your self-talk. You have to monitor the words that come out of your mouth that can poison your attitude, weaken your spirit, and drain your energy. You have to be careful with what you allow to come out of your mouth regarding yourself and your life. If all you do is complain about how bad something is, have a bad attitude, always feel like a victim, or even speak negativity over other people, you are only attracting more of that negative energy back to you. So, you can't be surprised when it seems like things aren't changing or seems to be getting worse. You may feel powerless, but you can do something about it, and it starts with getting your mouth right. Speak life into your situation, speak life into your dreams, and speak life into yourself. If you don't have anything good to say, just don't say anything. Sometimes, you have to wipe your tears, pick yourself up, get focused, and CLAIM WHAT YOU WANT. Speak it into existence. It may not feel like it, but if you keep saying it, and keep saying it, and keep saying it... it's only a matter of time before it raises your thinking, gets down into your spirit, and once it's alive on the inside, you will thrive on the outside.

CHANGE YOUR FOCUS

Many times, our lives are just a reflection of our focus. The things that we give the most attention to, consciously and subconsciously, will be what manifests in our lives. What are you focusing on? What's getting most of your attention? Are you focusing on how bad things are? Are you thinking about how you don't know how things are going to get any better? I understand. It's hard not to be mindful of your circumstances, especially when those circumstances are so far from what you want. Be that as it may, it's imperative that you monitor the things you're focusing on. You can't keep complaining about it. It will just make you feel worse, attract more things to complain about, and have no positive impact on the situation. When you focus on problems, you'll have more problems. When you focus on possibilities, you'll have more opportunities. What you want and the things you want to change are possible, but you have to focus on *those* possibilities. When you do, the opportunities you're looking for will present themselves. Stop being blinded by your own darkness. You don't have to wait. until you get to the end of the tunnel; you can be the light that gets you through.

ELIMINATION

Eliminate what doesn't help you evolve. Sometimes, finding the change that you are looking for doesn't consist of adding something to your life, but eliminating anything that doesn't grow you, add value to you, and/or help you to fulfill your purpose

YOUR SEASON

Your season of Breakthrough is coming! Don't wait on it, go out and seize it. Stop talking about it, and do something about it. Stop making excuses. Stop waiting for tomorrow. Don't run when you find out there is work involved. Trust yourself. Trust your abilities. Trust your strength, and remember everything that you had to go through to get here. You not only made it, you are better for it. So, stop letting what happens in your life be up to them; let it be up to you. These are *all your responsibility*. If you don't take action on it, there is no one else you can blame for your circumstances. You may not be in the position to do what you want to do, but you are in the position to DO SOMETHING.

RISE UP

I know it's hard. I know it's overwhelming. I know you are giving everything you've got, and it doesn't feel like enough. But this is your moment. Not a moment to wait for something to happen. This is your moment to decide. To CHOOSE. What you choose to DO will determine what happens next. Keep moving forward. Keep taking steps in the direction of your dreams. I don't care how big or small the steps are, just don't stop. You were born for a purpose. You were built for this, and you will rise. You will make a difference. You will change lives. And you will live your dreams!

BROKE BUT NOT BROKEN

Everyone you meet is fighting a battle that you don't know about. Some people are dealing with things you couldn't begin to understand. There is someone at this very moment who is thinking about giving up. They feel like if one more thing happens, they are going to be broken beyond repair. One of the saddest things in the world is a person who feels they have lost all hope. I have some news for anyone who has been there, or if you're there right now. The storm that you are going through didn't come to break you. That storm came to MAKE YOU. You don't know how amazing you are! You were built for this. Not to go through it, but to use it to become who you were meant to be. You are so special, and you don't even realize it. You aren't special because you have a few talents; you are special because YOU ARE YOU. And there is no one ever created who is like you. NO ONE! So, you may be hurt, you may be frustrated, and you may even feel broken, but even that pain has a purpose. That purpose is to break down your weak exterior and reveal the strength and potential of what is inside of you. You have the potential to create your vision of an extraordinary life. Let it out!

CREATE YOUR HAPPINESS

Happiness isn't a destination, it's a choice. Your power lies in your ability to be happy and complete with yourself without the need of any outside confirmation. Only you can control your own happiness. No one can give it to you or take it away. Happiness is yours to create in any moment. So, don't rely on anything or anyone for your happiness. If you do, those things will always be responsible for you being, or not being, happy. Happiness is an inside job. Decide to be happy. Find it inside, and change your life!

MIRROR, MIRROR

Admitting that you are struggling is important. Recognizing what you are struggling with is critical. But understanding why you are struggling and how to overcome it – that's the key to true growth. At some point, we have all come to a season in our lives when we come to a crossroad. We try to figure out how we came to this place in our lives. We start thinking about our experiences, our decisions, and our environment, trying to find the causes of our circumstances and our issues. One day, we recognize it staring at us in the mirror. There begins the true journey of self-discovery and understanding to let go of pain and counterproductive behaviors, and start becoming the remarkable, happy, successful, and fulfilled person we were meant to be.

FEAR TO GROW

Nothing great ever came from living in your comfort zone. You were never meant to be mediocre, and neither was your life. You can only grow when you allow yourself to experience new things and do something that you've never done before. So, always go with the choice that scares you the most because that is going to be the one to help you grow. Especially if it excites you and scares you at the same time - do that! Good is going with the flow. Greatness happens when you go against it.

JUST DO YOUR THING

The most amazing things happen when you invest in yourself. When you decide that you will just BE. You learn that you can't force anything in your life that doesn't fit. You learn that you don't have to chase people. You just have to become the kind of person that you want to attract. You learn that you don't have to compete with anyone. That you are your only competition, and your hard work will speak for itself. The things and people that belong in your life will be attracted to you. They will come and find you and stay. Just do your thing!

LIFE IS LIKE A BALLOON

We spend so much of our lives holding on to things that we should let go. Things that may be holding us down, or holding us back, from where we are supposed to go. Life is like a balloon…if you let go, you'll never know how high you can rise. Letting go isn't always an easy thing to do. In fact, it usually isn't easy at all. Ironically, we hold on the tightest to the things that we need to let go of the most. Sometimes, we need to let go of bad habits, destructive behaviors, negative environments, or toxic relationships. So, don't always think the thing holding you back is something you need to add to your life, because many times, it's something we need to let go.

NEW BEGINNINGS

A nd suddenly, you know… It's time to start fresh and trust the life you envisioned. The life you want isn't dead; it's just hidden behind the life you have. Don't keep recycling the same goals, the same pain, and the same excuses. Trust in the power of new beginnings.

DEFEND YOUR LIGHT

Surround yourself with people who feed the fire inside of you, not the people who try to throw water on it. Your success will be directly related to the people who you are around and the people who you communicate with on a daily basis. We have to be able to let go of people who aren't adding value to our lives. If they aren't adding, they are taking away. Defend your light with your life! Your happiness, your success, and your fulfillment depend on it.

BREATHE TO SUCCEED

When we become used to something, we can take it for granted... but the moment that thing becomes unavailable or limited, the value of it increases drastically. Our current circumstances determine what is truly valuable to us. If you were underwater, at the bottom of the ocean...money, cars, houses, etc. wouldn't matter. The ONLY thing that would matter to you is breathing. If you're not where you want to be right now in your life, think of it as being underwater. Your success, your dream, or wherever you want to be in your life is above that water. Sometimes, our lives feel like we're treading water. Sometimes, our lives feel like we're drowning...but we don't know how to swim. Like the expression, I'm just trying to keep my head above water. BUT the moment your craving to breathe becomes stronger than your willingness to give up, THEN you will be successful. When you ONLY have those two options, whether to push through those troubled waters to the top or to stop fighting and die...when you choose life... you choose to fight...you choose to keep swimming against all odds to get to the top...THEN YOU WILL BE SUCCESSFUL!

TIRED ENOUGH

One of the biggest motivators for change is just being tired of where you are, what you're going through, and your current circumstances. Tired of struggling. Tired of not being able to pay bills. Tired of where you live. Tired of a relationship. Tired of not being as fit as you want. JUST TIRED! The question is, how tired do you have to be to do something about it? How tired do you have to be to DECIDE that you are going to take whatever action, whatever changes, whatever training, whatever contacts, whatever moves you need to make to make your dreams happen? If you are too tired to put in the work it takes to make your dreams a reality, then you aren't tired enough of your current circumstances.

GRIND TO GROW

A re you grinding for show, or are you grinding to grow? People aren't going to see the type of work and sacrifice it takes to make your dreams a reality. They aren't going to see the late nights, the long hours, all the things that didn't work, all the obstacles that kept getting in your way, all those days it took everything in you not to quit. Don't do it for *them*, do it for YOU! Do it for those things in your life that are unconditionally important. The more you grow, the further you can go!

QUIT

If you're going to quit anything, quit making excuses, and quit waiting for the right time to live your best life. The time is NOW!

BORROWED TIME

To attempt and fail at living the life you actually want is more honorable than being successful at settling for whatever life gives you. Don't be afraid to live life on your own terms and on your own time. We have been conditioned to always be on *borrowed time* (on a job or making someone else rich) instead of controlling our own time. Even if you fail 100 times, you are doing more living than someone who is gaining material things, but someone else always controls their time, and they are afraid to live the kind of life they truly want.

OUT WITH THE OLD

I don't know what you're going through right now, but I do know that you are bigger, stronger, and smarter than your problem could ever be. Don't think you are...know you are. No matter the obstacles that have been keeping you from getting to where you need to be, this is your year. You have been in the darkness long enough. It's your time to shine. You made it through it all, and you're still here standing stronger than ever. You've seen it. Daydreaming, you have seen visions in your mind of what could be. No matter how hard things feel, you still know it's possible. It feels different this time. You have this feeling inside that life is about to change, and all of the things that you have been praying for are on the way. Believe it! Trust that feeling and embrace it! Have the courage to let go of the old and make way for the new breakthrough.

WAKE-UP CALL

I remember one of my mentors called me about ten times early one morning. I was sleeping, and when I finally called him back, he said, You must already be where you want to be! I said, Of course not; my alarm didn't wake me up on time. He got irritated and asked me, Why do you need an alarm to wake you up? If your dreams and goals aren't waking you up, then things must not be bad enough. You must be satisfied with where you are! You've been asleep your whole life! Let's just say I no longer needed an alarm to wake me up. I'M UP! So, stop saying that it's other people who are sleeping on your talent, your skills, and your gift. If you're not grinding with that gift every day, then you're sleeping on yourself. Wake up to your greatness! Don't sleep on your own success. If you're not where you want to be...if you're broke, if you're unhappy, if you're unfulfilled, and if you know that your life is meant for so much more... This is your wake-up call!

HARD PAST

Your past does not define you. In fact, the awesome, strong, and intelligent person that you have become is in spite of the mistakes, the tough times, and the pain. You made it. Who you are is the sum total of your life, the good AND the bad. As a matter of fact, it is because of the bad times. You are as strong as you are because of your past...those lessons...that wisdom...that experience... Use it! I guarantee that behind those people you admire, the people you look up to, and the most successful people in the world is a Hard Past.

FRIENDS WITH BENEFITS

The older you get, you realize how important it is to surround yourself with the right kind of people. If people aren't adding value to you, there's a chance they are having a negative impact on your life (or no positive impact). Surround yourself with people who are invested in your success. People who want to see you win. People who want to see you happy. People who not only want it but are willing to share the insight that they have to help you get there. They should believe in you, even at the times when you don't believe in yourself. They are there through the good and bad times and ride with you the whole journey. Those are Real Friends with Benefits!

PRIORITIZE

If it's truly important to you, you will find the time and find a way to make it happen, reach your goal, and follow your dream. They say if you don't find a way, you'll find an excuse. So often, I ask people what they want out of life. After they tell me, I ask what they are doing on a daily basis to take steps toward that goal. I usually get a long list of excuses. I know people who have several jobs, businesses, volunteer, are married, and have kids, but they make their happiness and life of success a priority.Don't live with what-ifs, maybes, and regrets. That's not living; that's existing. Live and create your own life!

BABY STEPS

Baby steps are steps, too. Any size step is progress. Moving forward is progress. Don't get comfortable with being still or allowing yourself to make an excuse to not do something just because you're not in an ideal situation. There is no perfect time. No matter where you're trying to go, if you keep moving forward, eventually you'll get there.

I AM BECAUSE I'VE BEEN

Y ou are strong because you have been weak. You are fearless because you have been afraid. You are wise because you have been foolish. No breakthroughs, triumphs, or victories are void of trials and pain. Every experience, good or bad, are opportunities for growth. But true growth isn't accomplished by the experience and just going through it. It is accomplished by taking the lessons learned from that experience and applying it. Hiding who you are isn't being strong. The ability to show your weakness and vulnerabilities in the face of what you truly want is true strength.

I

You're ready for a change in your life. You say you want better. You say you deserve better. You know there is more to this life for you. You've made some changes, but you're still not seeing them manifest at a level in your life that you truly want. There's no word more powerful to change your life than I. When you say I, you are taking 100% responsibility for your life. I empowers you to make a declaration of what you will accomplish and who you will become. I changes the game the moment you use it. Time to stop playing around and making excuses. Time is going to fly by faster than you think. What will you accomplish in these next 6 months that you have been putting off? What actions are you going to take that are going to get you closer to your goal? Ask yourself, and don't just talk about it, be about it!

FOOTPRINTS

Don't just walk the walk. Leave footprints big enough for others to follow. It's not enough to just exist. Your gifts, your experiences, and your time here should be reinvested in the generations to come. Your Purpose is bigger than a dollar amount or a title. There is something in this world that needs to be accomplished that ONLY YOU can do. Make your name count. Not the name on a piece of paper but that Name which is of the image in which you were created. You know you were meant for more. When they mention your name...what will they think about? The people that we idolize for changing the world still live on through their works and the impact they made. You were made to make an impact on this world...GO MAKE IT!

NO DISCOUNTS

Don't keep discounting yourself for people who don't know your worth. Don't allow yourself to keep settling for less just because others don't see your worth. You don't have to prove to anyone how great you are. If they don't see it, then it wasn't meant for them to see. You don't prove your value by saying it or putting on a mask to convince others. YOU determine your value by how you ALLOW others to treat you, and how YOU treat other people. You can be humble and priceless at the same time.

NEVER TOO LATE

It's never too late to become the person you were meant to be, and it's never too late to live the life you were meant to live. Don't ever think that your dreams and goals expire! No matter what anyone else says or what they are doing with their lives, they don't decide what you can do with your own life. Whatever you want to do, you can still do it. Whatever you want to have in your life, you can still have it. But you have to be brave enough to claim it. Say it! Tell someone, I'm going to start that business, I'm going to get that position, I'm going to get that degree. Remember, no matter your past, where you're from, or what they think you can do, you are the only person that can determine what your limitations are. If the Creator said it's for you...it's *for you*...regardless!

NO VACATION NEEDED

Create the kind of life that keeps you excited for Monday – Sunday, not just on Friday and Saturday. I don't think you were meant to just work a job that drags you through the week, just to have a day or two to recover and do it all over again. That's not living! You may get a week or two off a year to go on vacation, and a part of you doesn't even want to come back from the vacation (because you know it may be another year before you can do it again). So, when I say *create the kind of life you don't need a vacation from*, I bet you can feel that in my soul. You can see. You can imagine what that would be like. Allowing yourself to be subjected to a life that's way below what you deserve says something about how we feel about our self-worth, but more importantly, what we're willing to DO about it.

FIGHT

You have to fight some of the bad days to earn some of the best days of your life. Unfortunately, they are not all going to be good. Some days, you are going to feel like you wish you had a reset button, so you can start over and try again. The thing is, those are the days you really find out who you are. How you react to these things and how you let them affect you will have a big impact on what happens next. More importantly, what you do, or don't do, will determine the outcome at the end of the day. You can't let those days defeat you and turn into weeks, months, or years. You fight those days because you know there is something better in store. You know there is a blessing in that lesson.

FULL CIRCLE

Spend more time with people who are good for your personal growth and your mental health. Sometimes, we spend more time in situations and environments that hinder us rather than help us. If it costs you your peace, it's too expensive. That goes for people, as well. Your inner circle should stretch you, not stress you. They should hold you up, not hold you back. They should build you up, not bring you down. Sometimes, you may think you're just being a good friend, but all you ever hear is negativity and complaining. It gets to a point where these types of friends can affect your energy and your life. You want to be around people that challenge you in order to grow you, not people who are just a challenge to be around. Protect your energy and the energy you choose to be around! It's so important to where you are and where you're going.

DON'T LOOK BACK

There's no reason to look back when you have so much to look forward to. Your past doesn't define you, nor should it confine you from living your best life now. The things behind us have a way of creeping back into our lives. Sometimes, to possibly keep us from moving on and moving forward. Even if you've made mistakes in the past, that was the you *then* needing to grow into the you *now*. Take that lesson and learn from it by deciding to make a different choice. Past pain and unresolved emotions imprison our happiness like a ball and chain strapped to our leg. You can drag that pain into every relationship and every season of your life and not even realize it. Don't sabotage your present and your future. Let go, and just BE!

STEPPING-STONES

The obstacles that you are facing aren't roadblocks to your goals; they are stepping-stones to your success. It's a frustrating feeling when you feel like you're trying your hardest to do the *right* things, the right way and still feel like you can't catch a break. When you are on the path that you're supposed to be on, that path will take you to the kind of life that you envisioned for yourself. The *enemy* will try to throw everything at you but the kitchen sink to keep you from getting there. The place you are headed is the place where your greatness is waiting for you. Your dreams and goals are required to prepare you and test your dreams for authenticity. It's their way of making sure that you really want what you say you want, as bad as you say you want it. There is growth in those obstacles needed for you to be successful. There are lessons in overcoming those trials to best prepare you for what's coming. There are character-building circumstances in those dark times needed to become the person you are meant to be.

SEE THE WHOLE

Your path may be predestined, but it's not predetermined. Your purpose and your goal don't change, just the route you take to get there. If the first route didn't work, fine. The second route didn't work out? Okay. Even if the third doesn't work, you are still in good shape. Don't get so caught up in the mess that you forget the message. When we are able to get over ourselves, we are able to transcend the ego holding us back. Then, you will finally stop seeing the hole and see the whole.

REAL RECOGNIZE REAL

One day, something so crazy may happen in your life that it makes you stop, sit down, and really think about where you are in your life compared to where you want to be. Once you look in the mirror, and you don't recognize that reflection looking back at you, it's time for a change! You may even realize that crazy stuff has been going on around you for a while; you've just been so deep in it that you couldn't even see it (or were too scared see it). Now that you know something needs to change...what are you going do about it? Love yourself enough to take action, and believe in yourself enough to know you can do it!

FAITH IT 'TIL YOU MAKE IT

It can be frustrating to feel like you're doing everything in your power to get to where you want to be, but when you look around, you don't feel any better off than you were before. Sometimes, you don't even want to hear any it'll work out talk. You feel like you're all prayed out and sick and tired of being sick and tired. Wherever you are in your life right now...in this very moment...DECIDE that you are going to keep grinding until it happens. Believing is seeing, and you're not going to stop until you see what you saw. Believe, and keep moving forward. Believing is seeing!

ONLY BELIEVE

Your success isn't dependent on other people believing you can do it. Your success is ONLY based on if YOU BELIEVE you can do it. You don't *believe* by talking, you believe by DOING. You believe by taking the first step without seeing the second You believe by investing in yourself. You believe by going the extra mile that others won't. You believe by seeing something in yourself that only you and the Creator can see. You were never meant for settling and mediocrity. You weren't built like that. You are meant for greatness. Act like it!!

THE COST OF NOT FOLLOWING YOUR HEART

They say the cost of not following your heart is spending your life wishing you had. Don't get your *emotional heart* confused with your *spiritual heart*. The emotional heart is strong, but sometimes, it wants what it wants, regardless if it's the best for you or not. Your spiritual heart gives you vision. It gives you direction. Your spiritual heart is that voice inside that is always trying to push you in the direction of your destiny. The spiritual heart is what comforts you when your emotional heart is hurting. It is the thing that tries to lead you to where you need to be, even when it's the opposite of where you want to be. The answers to your prayers and dominant thoughts are *downloaded* into your spiritual heart. When you're waiting on a sign or an answer, not realizing that the little voice inside has been trying to tell you all along. So, when you keep seeing this vision in your head about what you can accomplish, when you keep feeling inspired and getting these great ideas but fail to act on them, and every time you tell yourself to follow your gut, it's your spiritual heart that is talking to you. Don't spend your life looking for answers that you already know, and don't spend your life looking for something that you've already found. Time is your most precious gift. Don't waste it! Follow Your Heart.

ASK YOURSELF

We all have those moments in our lives when we don't feel like ourselves anymore. Something feels off! When we look at certain aspects of our lives, we're not happy (career, relationship, physique). Sadly, many times, we get so worn out that we settle because we're tired of being disappointed. We start to feel like the life we have is the best it's going to get. If you feel that way right now, it means that you are not in alignment with what you really want in your life. Ask yourself... How do I feel right now? Why do I feel like this? What do I really want? What makes me happy? What is holding me back? What can I do about it? You can't stay still and expect to move forward.

MAKE ROOM

Contrary to popular belief, there is way more than enough (money, resources, accomplishments) to go around! By uplifting others, you're not going to be less successful. Someone else's success is not going to keep you from being successful. If you are fortunate to be in a position to help someone else get there... DO it! You were once in their shoes. You know what it feels like. You know what it's like to go through that struggle of figuring it out. More than likely, someone helped you out, gave you some advice, put in a good word, or even gave you an opportunity. Don't build higher fences to keep people out, make room at the table to let people in.

REMIND YOURSELF

Sometimes, just trying to deal with the constant struggles of everyday life can make you feel like you're losing control...and as time goes on, you feel like you're losing yourself. It's a terrible feeling to not feel like yourself anymore. To feel like the things that made you unique and special - the things that made you excited about life - are fading away. We all can forget sometimes, but the key is to always remind yourself who you really are. Remind yourself of just how amazing you are! Remind yourself that you were specifically and meticulously designed for a purpose that ONLY YOU can give to the world. Remind yourself that your potential is only limited by your mind, your imagination, and your own limitations. Remind yourself that the life you envisioned for yourself is not only possible, but that life is yours. Claim it! Always remember who you are and what you're fighting for. When you remember, the game changes.

LET EM' KNOW

L ife comes at us so fast! We're so focused on trying to survive, trying to progress, and trying to better our lives that we can take some things for granted. There are some people in your life who ground you, have your back, support your happiness, believe in you, want to see you win, and gives you their shoulder when you need it. Even though those kinds of people never do it because they want anything, letting those people know that you appreciate them goes a long way.

SEEK FIRST TO UNDERSTAND

When people are going through something or they've been hurt, they want to be heard. But most of all, they want to be understood. If someone you care about is talking to you from the heart, don't just listen so you can have something to say back. If that's the case, you're not listening at all. So, the next time someone you care about comes to talk to you about something that is really bothering them, put yourself in their shoes, look them in the eyes, feel their energy, and digest the words coming out of their mouth. Even if you don't know how to respond immediately after, the fact that you are really trying to understand what they are feeling and where they are coming from will mean more to them than anything you can say.

JUMP

S top talking yourself out of opportunities because you don't feel like you're ready yet. It's time to jump. You are ready now! The older you get, the more you're going realize that when life comes at you, it comes at you fast. The years you felt like you once had started to feel like days that were going by too fast. In the blink of an eye, the life that you know could be turned upside down. All the things you wish you had done, wish you said, chances you should have taken, and things you shouldn't have taken for granted become the most important things. You've waited long enough, and you've made enough excuses. You have cheated yourself out of the opportunities, happiness, and fulfillment for too long. Stop waiting to live...now is your time. Jump!

IT'S OKAY

It's okay to be tired, but don't give up. You might feel like you just can't catch a break. Every time you turn around, there's something else you have to deal with. That stuff is draining! It drains you emotionally, psychologically, and physically. It's okay... have your moment. Get it out. Breathe. Even if you get knocked down, it'll still be okay. But if it's two weeks later, and you're still down...that's a problem. Get up! Dust yourself off and keep going. It's all working out for your good. Keep moving forward.

TIRED

You may feel tired, not because you've done too much, but because you've done too little of the things that mean the most to you. We spend too much time being busy and not enough time being effective and fulfilled. You can be doing a lot of things, but if those things don't make you happy... If they don't make you feel alive... If they don't bring you closer to your dreams... Why even do them? Don't say because you have to! I've tried to convince myself that was true, too, but at the end of the day, you always have a CHOICE. I'm not saying that the choices are always easy because they usually aren't. But, it's usually the hardest choices that lead us to the place we've been struggling to get to. Do more of the things that really matter, and save your energy from the things that are stealing your joy instead of adding value to your life.

DON'T DAMAGE YOUR SOUL

Temporary pain to your heart is not worth permanent damage to your soul. You can't keep making excuses for people who maliciously hurt you, demean you, and tear you down. How they treat you is usually not even about you, it's about their dissatisfaction with themselves. Every time you place yourself into that toxic environment, you are subjecting your soul and your spirit to more damage. That kind of damage is difficult to heal and has a lasting effect on you for years to come. The decisions you may have to make will be difficult, but you are so worth it.

IT'S TIME FOR A PROMOTION

You are the CEO of your own life. It's time to start acting like it. You've been acting like an associate, and you're supposed to be running it. So, stop letting other people run you, telling you how you can live, what you can have, and what you can accomplish. How are you going be the assistant of your own life?

Letting someone else control you and tell you how to handle your own business and monopolize your valuable time keeps you from progressing. Do you know the greatness that's inside of you? If you don't know, NOW you know. It's time for a promotion!

STORMY WEATHER

We will all face storms in our lives that feel like they have come with the purpose of breaking us down, tearing us apart, and causing as much pain as possible. Not all storms are destructive. Sometimes, the only way we can see clearly is to be humbled by life. When you get knocked down enough times or hard enough, it's going to make you look at some things with a new perspective. You're going to realize the true strength of just who you are looking at in the mirror. You're going to question your priorities, your decisions, your environment, and the people in your life. When that storm finally passes, some things may be broken, some things may be destroyed, but what remains clears the path for you to get to where you need to go.

BINGE-WORTHY

If you can make time to binge-watch a show, then you can make time to binge on things that feed your spirit, fuel your dreams, and pushes you toward your goals. We've all been guilty of this in some form or fashion. The number one excuse for why we can't do the things we say we need to do to accomplish our goals is that we don't have time. We're so busy. We'll take a whole day to binge watch a show but don't binge on the things that actually add value to our lives. While it's true, we can be extremely busy with so much going on...that old saying still holds true. We will make time for what we really want to make time for. Give yourself, your goals, your dreams, and the things that are most important to you that priority.

THE CIRCLE OF SUCCESS

There are five types of people you want to surround yourself with. The inspired. The passionate. The motivated. The grateful. The open-minded. Inspirational people make you want more from your life. They inspire you to be more and dream bigger. Passionate people are energetic about life and the things that they deeply care for. You can't help but feel that passion when you're in their presence. Motivated people fuel you by pushing themselves toward their goals, and they make you want to do the same. Grateful people have a calming energy. They remind you of what's really important by being unconditionally thankful. Open-minded people are easy to talk to. They are always looking to broaden their horizons, and they are able to be objective with you without judging you.

EMERGENCY

Make your dreams an emergency as if your life depends on it... because it does. Sometimes, we don't think about what it means when we don't chase our dreams with everything we have. Think about how your life will be different when you're living your dream. Think about all the things you'll be able to do, places you'll be able to go, how your family's life will change, and the freedom you'll be able to have when you make your dreams a reality. Live every day like your dreams are an emergency. Grind with a sense of urgency. If you're tired of how things are, and you want them to change, make accomplishing your goals THE priority.

SATISFIED

Unfortunately, many of us have been conditioned to accept a mediocre life. We know it's not what we want or what we deserve, but yet, we accept it. When you accept a life below your vision, you are accepting it. You accept it when you know you deserve better, but you don't do anything about it. Even if you try to do something about it, and it doesn't initially work out, it isn't a sign to quit. It means you need to take what you learned from that experience and try something else. When we continually complain but fear doing what it takes to change our circumstances, we turn that into our reality. So, it's not always what happens, or doesn't happen, it's only what we accept as our truth. Only you know what your truth is. If your life isn't in alignment with what fulfills you and makes you happy, then it isn't your truth. Deep down, your spirit isn't satisfied. It's hungry for the life you want. It's hungry for the life you deserve! You are more than your past, more than your circumstances, and you are more than any problem that you may be facing. Don't be satisfied until whatever is in your heart is what you're living in your life.

EVERYTHING HEALS

No matter how much pain you're in. No matter how much hurt you have in your heart. No matter how bad things seem. Bad times don't last. It may not feel like it right now, but you were made to withstand more than you could ever imagine. These things didn't come to break you, they are only meant to show you that they can't break you. No matter how bad the wound feels, it will heal. Every part of you is amazing at healing itself. Everything heals. Your body heals. Your mind heals. Your heart heals. Your soul repairs itself. No matter how dark it gets at night, or how cold it gets in the winter, the sun always comes back. Always! And with it comes new light that brings new life to everything it touches. So, no matter what you feel you've lost - happiness, love, peace - it will always come back to you if you let it. The very things that felt like they were going to break you were only preparing you for your BREAKthrough.

ISLAND OF EXCELLENCE

Become an island of excellence in a sea of mediocrity. You can be great all by yourself no matter where you are and no matter what everyone else is doing around you. Don't sacrifice your potential just because others around you can't see it in you and choose not to see it in themselves. Your excellence will inspire them, motivate them, or make them take an honest look at themselves. But either way, refuse to settle for anything less than the full expression of your gifts, talents, and purpose.

DUALITY

Too many times we are told that our self-awareness is singular. Meaning, you either have to be one thing, or you have to be the other. Like you can only be strong or weak, happy or sad, whole or broken... It's just not possible, and it's not how we're built. So, don't let society, or your ego, convince you that at any time, you can only be on one level to be in a good place. Life is about DUALITY! Duality is the ability to acknowledge a state of being and a state of becoming at the same time. You can acknowledge your strength and still be aware of your sensitivities. You can learn while making mistakes. You can grow while walking through obstacles. You can heal and still appreciate the support.

CHANCE OR CHOICE

You're not always going to have someone to motivate you. Some days, you're just not going to be feeling it. The most unexpected things can happen at what feels like the worst times.

The main difference between you and the people you aspire to emulate is Choice. Those people aren't necessarily any stronger than you or smarter than you, but they made a decision that no matter what life brings, their destination will not change. So, the difference between where you are and where you want to be isn't chance...it's choice. You decide!

NOT ALLOWED

Don't allow yourself to be empty for people who won't fill you. Don't bring yourself down for people who don't lift you up. Don't continue to walk a thousand miles for people who will only walk past you. Kindness can be your strength, and being treated as less doesn't have to be your weakness.

NEVER CHANGE

No matter how bad you want to stop being the nice one, how bad you want to stop being the one to take the high road, or how bad you want to hurt those who hurt you, *don't let anybody change you*. Sometimes, we feel like we aren't any better off for trying to do the right thing. We may feel like we are weak or letting people get the best of us because we don't treat them the same way they treat us. Sometimes, you get so fed up that you just want to give them a taste of *their own medicine*. Just so they can see how it feels. At the end of the day, it's not you...and it's not worth it. The reason why you don't react that way or treat them that way speaks to the quality of your character. Don't reduce yourself for someone else. Don't feel the need to lower yourself to their level because they aren't on your level in the first place. If you have to remove yourself from the situation, do it. If you have to speak your peace, speak it. If you see that something has to change, change it. Don't let it change you.

KNOW GPS

Navigating our personal growth requires that we learn to be self-aware. Aware of what's going on around us, but mostly, aware of what's going on inside of us. It's not always other people who are holding us back. Many times, we are the ones who need a paradigm shift, an attitude adjustment, and a reality check. True growth and real change only come when we hold ourselves accountable and constantly make adjustments when needed.

EMPTY CUP

As much as we have to give, there is only so much we can do. You are only one person. And as amazing as you are, you can't be everything to everybody. You give so much of yourself away and wonder why you feel empty inside. The only way you can even have anything to give is to first give to yourself. It's not selfish, but rather, necessary if you want to be of any use to the people you care about and the people who care about you. You have to fill your cup before you can pour into anyone else's. If your cup is empty, you have absolutely nothing to pour. You have nothing to give. Most importantly, you will have nothing to give to yourself. So above all, practice self-love by pouring into yourself first. Do more of the things that make you smile, make you laugh, and make you happy. Make your dreams a priority. Exercise more, and eat healthier. Meditate more, and stress less. Express yourself more, and don't bottle up your emotions. You can't be everything to everyone else while being nothing to yourself. The better you are to yourself, the better you are able to give to the most important things in your life.

SHADOW OF FEAR

G et out of the shadow of fear, and stand in the light of your greatness. Stand in your truth and release whatever is holding you back. Your dreams and fear cannot exist in the same place.

SELF-LOVE

Self-love isn't a destination. It is a combination of a state of being and a state of becoming. It is a life-long journey filled with lessons, mistakes, and revelations. This is so important to understand so that when life gets hard, you are better prepared to navigate the obstacles and come out of it stronger than before.

BORROWED TIME

If you don't claim power over your life, then it's guaranteed that someone else will. Stop being reactive and be proactive. Don't wait for something to happen before you take control of your own life. That means if you don't take action on the things you want to change, if you don't take your livelihood into your own hands, and if you don't reclaim freedom over your time, then you give permission for someone else to do that for you. If could be your job, it could be in your relationship, or it could be the opportunities you have to provide for your family. You are responsible. You don't have to do anything that is not in alignment with what you want, what you need, and what you deserve.

READY OR NOT

To truly and completely love yourself may mean that you have to love certain people from a distance. Don't keep sacrificing your own happiness and self-fulfillment in an attempt to save situations that are already dead or are not serving what you need in your life. That doesn't always mean letting go but may mean turning loose. You can't force anyone to be something they are not ready to be. No matter how bad you want it for them, no matter how much you think things would be different if they changed, no matter how much you think a certain thing will save them. Your intentions are good, but no one can change until *they* decide they are ready.

STANDARDS

Be honest with people about who you are, what you want, and how you expect to be treated. Standards only scare people who are not meant for you.

TOO GROWN

Don't continue to sacrifice yourself for people you have outgrown. Many relationships/friendships are seasonal. That person was only meant to be active in your life at a specific time, for a specific length of time, and for a specific reason. I know it's difficult to accept, but it's necessary to understand to not only get past it but to grow from it. Those relationships can become so toxic that in some ways, they are taking away from who you are and who you are meant to become. Don't sacrifice your happiness, your success, and your potential for people who don't add any value to your life.

APPLICATION ACCEPTED

Most of the time, it's not our beliefs that hold us back, it's our lack of application of those beliefs. Taking action puts us in alignment with our Faith, but when we don't...what does it say about what we truly believe? If you feel defeated at this moment, don't accept that you can't do anything about it. Instead, look at the situation as an opportunity to become better. What have you learned from it? Defeat is temporary. It's only permanent if you accept it and give up. Use it as nothing more than a point to start from and a foundation to build on.

START SOMETHING

You can start with nothing and still start something. Don't think that you have to have everything figured out before you start working toward your goals. Even if you don't have the money or resources, you can still start saving and researching, and find out exactly what you're going to need to make it happen. Don't make the excuse of not knowing how because more than in other time in history, you can access just about any information and find appropriate training with a few clicks. The point is, you don't need to have it all figured out, or be in the perfect place, to start. Everything starts with an idea, a clear vision, and consistent actions toward a definite purpose. You're not waiting for things to happen, they are waiting for you.

GIVE YOURSELF

Nothing sabotages your happiness and growth like regret and grief. Give yourself permission to let go and heal. Even if you feel broken, you can love yourself back together again. Hidden inside of that hurt is the power to find the peace that you need. Being down doesn't make you defeated, and being hurt doesn't make you damaged. You are complete even when you feel a void, and you are whole even if you feel like part of yourself has vanished. Give your heart a place to heal and your spirit a place to grow.

THE VALUE OF WORTH

Not everyone who gets you deserves you. There's no greater tragedy than settling for less in love and less in life. When you settle for less in one, it means you are settling for less in the other. It's one thing to say you know your worth, but it's a totally different thing to know your value. Anyone can put a price tag on something and state that it's worth a certain amount. Especially when we are being told that we are only worth the sum of our material possessions. Even the wages that you are paid from your employer are based on how much they feel the services that you provide are worth to them. No one can ever decide your worth as long as you know your value. You can't even put a number on value. Value implies significance and importance. Value is assessed by how much something means. It speaks to emotion. It speaks to the connection. Those are two things that can't be measured, they can only be felt. Knowing your true value is what makes you irreplaceable. Value is a thing that can't be quantified by numbers, money, status, race, looks, size, or background. You're not valuable because you are this or that; you are valuable simply because you are you. There is no one in this world like you, and that makes you more special and more precious than you could ever imagine.

Breathe that in, and embrace it. Never again will you diminish your own value just because others may fail to see it, understand it, acknowledge it, or appreciate it. If they appreciate your value, you will never have to chase them. If they truly understand how unique you are, you will never have to convince them. Once you start to love yourself fully and understand the nuances that make you valuable, the things that you are looking for will start looking for you.

BE YOU

You are different. You are unique. You are special. You were created to be exactly who you are, and who you are isn't like them. Who you are is just like you. Exactly who you were meant to be. So, take off that mask that looks like everyone else, change that mind that thinks like everyone else, and change that behavior that does what everyone else is doing. You don't have to be like them. You don't have to hide. You don't have to suppress what's inside of you. Don't spend your life trying to make others comfortable by sacrificing your own comfort. You are who you are, and who you are is a beautifully unique spirit born for greatness. Greatness doesn't come from fitting in, it comes from standing out. Greatness doesn't come from going down their path, greatness comes from creating your own. True success doesn't come because you are better than you were yesterday. Success comes from finding the truest and fullest expression of yourself and expressing it. Stop minimizing who you are to accommodate the insecurities of others. Don't you look down. Keep your head high! The things that make you different are the very things that will make you great. Embrace them. Nurture them. Master them. Learn how to express them in a way that brings you joy and gives something back to the world at the same time.

So, take off the mask. Choose yourself. Choose your destiny. Choose your happiness. Be proud. Be you.

MOMENT OF SILENCE

L earn how to express them in a way that brings you joy and
gives something back to the world at the same time. So, take
off the mask. Choose yourself. Choose your destiny. Choose your
happiness. Be proud. Be you.

THE AFFIRMATION POWER

I was made in the image of the Creator of the heavens and earth. I was born with a purpose. A purpose that only I can fulfill. The world needs something that only my unique self can provide. I will master my special combination of gifts and talents. I know what I am is a gift from God, but what I become is my gift to God. There is no one, nor will there ever be, anyone like me. I was given a vision in my mind and in my spirit for what I can accomplish. I know that I have the ability to create my own life based on that vision. I understand that this life will not be given to me, I must claim it. I claim it by the thoughts that I think, the energy that I release, the words that come out of my mouth, and I bring those into the physical world with my actions. I know I will fall, but I will not stay down. I know I will have failure, but I will fail. I know that I will get tired, but I will press on. I take full responsibility for my life. I won't blame anyone for my circumstances. I will use my stumbling blocks as stepping stones to my success. I know the key to my evolution will be to never stop learning. I will seek knowledge, especially knowledge of self. I understand that I am my greatest investment. The more I pour into myself, the more I can pour into others and into the world. I understand that I can't control everything that happens, but I can control what I do about it. My power is knowing that I have the ability to change my life at any moment, reinvent myself as needed to grow, and try to impact the world around me through the fullest expression of my potential. My power is my individuality. I will continue to learn how to be the best version of myself. I know that it is never too late to become who I am meant to be, so I will remain in a state of becoming until everything I've envisioned becomes a reality. I am Power!

DRIVING ON EMPTY

When you are feeling low, give yourself time to fill yourself back up. Low on energy, low on time, or low on love. No matter how bad you feel, you need to keep going forward. It's time to take a step back. You won't get far with no fuel, and you can't fill others when you're empty. Stop, and take a deep breath. Take a moment to just be. The most important thing you can do for your dreams and for those who care about you is to take good care of yourself.

BEAUTIFUL

Don't allow other people to project their idea of beauty on you. Your skin is beautiful. Your hair is beautiful. Your body is beautiful. Just because we live in a culture that was shaped by individuals who don't know where you're from, don't know what you're capable of, and don't know who you are, their projections aren't your truth, and they don't have to become your reality.

YOUR TRUTH

Don't be afraid of your truth. You were not given a spirit of fear. Your truth is what defines you. It's the secret to harnessing and understanding your true power. Your greatness is in your truth. Learn your truth, know your truth, and embrace your truth. You will no longer shrink yourself for a box you don't fit in. You will no longer omit pieces of your truth for the comfort of others. Your truth does not require acceptance, but your truth demands respect. Your truth is what made you the person you are today. Your destiny is within your truth. Your potential is hidden inside your truth. Whatever you are and whatever you will be, your truth will set you free.

UNLEARNING

Unlearning is a part of growth. As we grow up, sometimes we are taught some unhealthy behaviors, some bad habits, and some things that are just wrong. No matter what you were taught, you can unlearn those things that are not aligned with your spirit. They don't have to define you. Even though that may have been who you were then, it doesn't have to be who you are today. You don't become who you were taught to be, you become who you choose to be. Unlearning is a part of the journey to get to the destination that you seek.

LOVED BACK TO LIFE

L ove is a powerful thing. As powerful as love is, we can't depend on other people to do what we are unable to do for ourselves. Love ourselves unconditionally. When we lose that love, we feel like we've lost a piece of ourselves. Every time we've allowed love in, and that love gets lost, we start to feel like as long as that love is gone, we can never be the same again. At that moment, we feel so broken, like a part of us just died. Then we look for someone whose love is so strong, that they can love back to life. That their love will sweep up the broken pieces of our heart and put it back together. To love us so hard that they fill the big void in us and make us feel whole again. As bad as we want that to happen, it's just not going to happen that way. No one can love you back to life. You are the only one who can do that for yourself. Everything begins and ends with you, but you have to first give yourself permission. You have to allow yourself to love. Give yourself permission to forgive, and allow yourself to let go. Give yourself permission to live, and allow yourself to breathe. Give yourself permission to accept, and allow yourself to see what's inside of you. Know that true love can never be lost. Know that God has never stopped loving you. Know that you have all the love inside you that you will ever need.

You have enough love to find the pieces and put them back together even better than before. To want to give love is honorable, wanting to receive love is natural, but wanting to be love is who you already are. Give yourself to yourself. The work isn't up to anyone else, it is always up to you.

OVERFLOW

Who says you have to live empty? You are allowed to be full. Full of joy. Full of love. Full of life. You are allowed to do the things that fill you and fulfill you until it overflows. Overflows into everything that you do and everywhere that you go. That energy is allowed to overflow into the people around you. You are not meant to live being half of yourself. Half-happy or half-loved. Half-fulfilled is not fulfilled. Live your whole life striving to be your whole self.

SEEDS OF THOUGHT

You are what you think, and what you become is sum total of your thoughts. Nothing can grow without first being a seed, and no seed can take root without first being planted. The quality of your thoughts will either make you or unmake you, but the choice is always yours. Master your thoughts, mold your character, make your conditions, shape your environment, and create your destiny. Your mind is like a garden, but it will bring forth a harvest of abundance or useless weeds depending on how it is cultivated or neglected. So, as long as you believe that you are a product of your outside conditions, you will never realize that you are the creative power.

GOAL MINER

The most precious jewels are only obtained through vigorous mining and searching. You can find every truth if you are willing to dig deep into the mine of your soul. The soul attracts what it loves, but it can also attract what it fears. Circumstances do not make you, they only reveal you to yourself. Who you choose to be in those moments will determine how, and if, those circumstances change. So, you don't attract what you want, you attract what you are. The divinity that formed you lives inside of you. It is your very self. One receives what they want and pray for when their thoughts and actions are in harmony. This is your story, and you are the author of your destiny.

THE FINISH LINE

The race to your life of success and fulfillment is a marathon, not a sprint. Just like a marathon, when you start your journey toward the finish line, you are excited. You feel good about the opportunity, and you feel strong enough to get to your destination. As you continue to run the race, you start to get tired and weary. The finish line now feels so far away. A part of you is ready to just give up and stop running. In that moment, when you're ready to give up, you get a boost of energy from somewhere. Your adrenaline kicks in and gives you renewed energy to keep going. You suddenly feel a little better and keep pushing forward. Then, you get to a point where your muscles start to cramp. Your body feels like it's going to give out on you. You start to feel like if you don't stop running, your body is going to shut down. When all hope seems lost, you dig deep down and decide. You decide that you are going to trust yourself, trust your body, and trust your journey. You refuse to let anything keep you from getting to that finish line. Suddenly, there's no more pain and no more pressure. Your body goes into cruise control, and it feels like you're running effortlessly. You have tapped into something remarkable inside of you. A person who is able to keep pushing through pain, keep pushing through adversity, and keep pushing through feeling like giving up will surely be successful and make it to the finish line.

THE POWER OF VISION

Nothing disciplines your life like vision. Vision controls your decisions and choices. Once you know where you're going, you know which roads won't take you there. Vision defines your *what to do* in life. Vision shows your destination and your destiny. It's easy to say no to things that don't coincide with your vision. Stress comes from not knowing what to do. Vision alleviates that stress. Vision is how God speaks to you. It is how you receive the revelation (reveal-ation) of your prayers. Vision is the dream that won't go away. A desire that won't leave. The thing that makes you angry because you keep seeing it, but you haven't gotten there yet. Sight is the ability to see things as they are, but vision is the ability to see things as they could be.

TODAY, I'M READY

As you look in the mirror, understand that the only person holding you back from your destiny is looking back at you. So, when you see them every morning, you tell them: Today, I may not be where I think I should be, but I am where I'm supposed to be. So, I am grateful for everything that I have and everything that I am. Today, I am, and will be, better than I was yesterday. Today, I will take the first steps to be who I want to become, regardless of the challenges that are in front of me. Today, I will take action on a plan I've created to get to the place I want to be, in spite of my pride and in the face of my fears. Today, I will declare with my words, claim with my thoughts, and believe with my heart that the victory is already won. I'm ready!

A MATTER OF CHOICE

There comes a point in our lives when we stop making excuses and start backing up our words. We can't keep doing the same things and expect things to change. We can't keep living in fear, playing it safe, staying in our comfort zone, and keep turning down opportunities to grow. There will never be a perfect time, and your situation will never be ideal. Your moment is now. The most frustrating thing that can happen is that when you look up this time next year, you're in the exact same place. So, what you want is never a matter of chance, it's always a matter of choice.

SPACE

Showing up for yourself may mean stepping back from others. Give yourself the space needed to recharge, reconnect, and refocus. Understand that it has nothing to do with them and everything to do with what you need. Be unapologetic about doing what's best for you. It's nothing personal, and those who truly care about you will understand.

POISON

D on't give anyone the power to infect your life with their negativity. Just as you are always giving energy out, you are also always receiving it. So, you have to protect it at all costs. Some people will find joy in trying to bring chaos into your life. Some people won't bring negative energy on purpose. But whether it's in the form of consistent complaining or always seeing the worse in every situation, that energy can spread to you. You can't allow toxic people to steal your joy, steal your power, or steal your peace. Keep your heart and your spirit away from poisonous people.

THE DESTROYER OF GREATNESS

The Destroyer is the greatest enemy to everything that you want to accomplish in your life. He comes to rob your future, steal your potential, and kill your dreams. The Destroyer can take the strongest person and render them powerless. He whispers in your ear in an attempt to make you avoid the life you want and settle for less than you're worth. The Destroyer will make you feel like you've failed, even before you've started. In order to defeat this beast, you have to tame it. You have to look him straight in the eyes with unwavering faith and supreme confidence. With every attack he renders (and he will attack), you must remind yourself that you are in control of your own destiny. You must not betray your potential, weaken your abilities, and ignore your purpose. Take control of your mind and direct your own thoughts toward the path of opportunity, adventure, happiness, love, passion, and fulfillment. You will be reminded that you are the master of your fate. You are the controller of your destiny. You are the key to your own success. You don't just possess power, you are power. You were meant for more. You are more. You were built for greatness. Declare that you will not be defeated, and you won't stop until the victory is won.

TAKE OFF

Your success in life rests on your relentless ability to get up and chase your dreams with fire each day. You have to attack each day with intent, with reason, and with power. You can't approach each day aimlessly and expect your goals, your dreams, and your life to hit the target. Set your path, and your way will be made straight. Don't spend your time, utilize every waking minute. Spending will only keep you poor of progress, poor of advancement, and poor of success. Rather, utilize every second of your twenty-four hours to beat your goals into submission. Take out all of your pain on creating a life big enough to erase that hurt. Take out all of your frustration on having a relentless work ethic that will not be denied. Mediocre people react to the day, but the great people are constantly preparing for it. Every day should be a step forward. No matter how big or small the step is, don't stop moving forward. Don't fear failing, fear being in the same place for years. Your journey and your destination are predestined, but you have to choose to take it. First, you may have to crawl until you're able to walk, but once you start running, you will eventually take off and be on a non-stop flight to that amazing place that's waiting for you.

EMOTIONS

True enlightenment comes when we realize that happiness is a choice, sadness is a choice, anger is a choice, and love is a choice. Every mind state that a human is capable of is readily available and can be generated by the will in our minds. This revelation is the key to emotional breakthrough. This is not to diminish the power of outside sources that influence the appearance of these emotions, but it is in the realization of our ability to choose is where we find our power.

CHOOSE

Seize your truth. Use the full capacity of your abilities to become your higher self and do your highest good. Express who you truly are and pursue the goals you find meaningful. Be strategic when considering your direction, and make sure whatever direction you take adds value. The choice should add value to your life or add value to the lives of others, but hopefully, it adds value to both. Figure out what makes you feel the most alive and what gives you the greatest sense of fulfillment. Never let your mind or the thoughts of others limit your aspirations and intentions. Be bold and unwavering, calling forth the greatest parts of your character. So, in the eyes of others you may appear lucky or chosen, but in fact, it was because you decided to choose.

MEET LIFE WITH POWER

Believe it or not, you were meant to have a divinely inspired experience in this life. Too many of us have become slaves to the hardships of life and have mentally, emotionally, and physically checked out of our own lives. We are not in tune with the energy and the circumstances around us and don't understand our responsibility to impact them. We become ungrateful for the blessings we have and mentally distance ourselves so that our minds are preferably somewhere else. Our life force is dwindling to a fraction of what it once was. Our life's purpose feels lost, unaccounted for, and unlived. Life is not meant to be a series of unwanted experiences, life is meant to be experienced to its fullest power. In order to be the director of this experience, we must bring the full power of our conscious minds into the present. We must choose to feel the life going on around us and sense when we are not aligned with the energy that we need. Remember that all we love of life is now. All we seek is here. All that we need to create the experiences that we want are available to us at this moment. Everything that truly matters to you is available now for you to order from the menu of your mind. Life will continue to happen, but we must decide how we will direct life's energy in each moment. When we learn to direct our awareness and power, inadequacies disappear, and the vitality of the fullness of life will return.

LIFE UNNOTICED

Don't miss the sunrise and sunsets for the trees. Don't allow yourself to be numb to your own feelings for hours or days at a time. Don't hold your head down and miss the smiles on the faces of the people who love you. Don't miss every opportunity to be there for yourself, so that you won't miss the desperate times when someone may need you the most. Don't miss experiencing the seasons locked behind doors or hiding behind the pain. You'll miss the blooming of the flowers, the warmth of the sun, and the crispness of the spring air. Don't be so busy thinking about yesterday or tomorrow that you miss the magic of today. Life is not meant to be half-engaged or half-lived. Life is meant to lived fully and completely. Don't let key moments pass you by because you locked the door on life. Your reality is only here, only now, and you have to choose to be in it, and live it.

YOUR GIFT

You probably have talents that people don't know about. You have gifts that you don't get to use. Maybe you even have degrees and certifications that you have earned, but you don't even have a job that utilizes them. At the end of the day, you have to follow your spirit. If you have a gift that you love and are passionate about, don't let anyone tell you that you can't be successful using it. Don't let them tell you that you can't build a career or a business from the talent that makes you feel like you're fulfilling your purpose. You can literally be a millionaire doing just about anything! I've seen it. What's the use of working hard and having money if you're miserable? Of course, do what you have to do, but that doesn't mean you have to give up on your gift. Your gift will make a way for you. Nurture it, master it, and bless the world with it.

ALIVENESS

Right now, at this moment, you may be standing in the space between where you are and where you want to be. That space can feel like you're standing on a long back road at night with nothing around you, and you're trying to figure out if you should go back the way you came, stay where you are and wait for someone to help you, or keep going in the direction you were headed. Right now, you not only have the ability but also the responsibility, to exercise your God-given freedom to live your life at its highest level. The moment you claim your ability to co-create with your spirit, your mind begins to dissolve the false boundaries that previously kept you from doing so. You have a gift to give to the world that is beyond what your mind may accept. So, commit to discovering and expressing that life by creating creativity, and what will emerge is living and expressing from the deepest parts of your being. This is real Aliveness!

CELEBRATE YOURSELF

Today, you need to celebrate yourself. Too many times, we are so focused on what we haven't accomplished that we don't give ourselves enough credit for what we have. Celebrate that you've made it through your past, and you came out of it better. You've done some pretty amazing things and made the most of what you had. It wasn't always easy, but you did it. Don't wait for others to acknowledge what you've done or to validate your successes. You validate them by acknowledging yourself. You may not be where you want to be, but thank God, you're not where you used to be. Believe it or not, many people don't have the opportunities that you have. For that, you should be grateful. Even if no one else recognizes you, sees you, or acknowledge your journey, you should recognize yourself. Celebrate who you've become and especially who you are becoming!

LET LOVE BACK IN

In order to let love back in, I have to allow myself to be open again. I can't close myself off and expect what is meant for me to find me. I won't allow hurt to win. Time will pass, and scars will heal, but I will remain capable of loving and being loved. I will continue to be, and I will continue becoming. Pain won't steal the best of me. As hard as it is, I have to let go of the baggage I'm dragging into my happiness. I know that they both can't exist in the same place. My past will no longer hold me back from the life that is meant for me. I have lived, I have learned, and I am better for it. I am determined that nothing will stop my happiness. Nothing will keep me from the life that's meant for me. I've been through too much, and I've come too far. My life of love, happiness, and fulfillment belongs to me.

PATIENCE IS A VIRTUE

You have to be just as patient with yourself as you expect others to be with you, and as you try to be with others. Everyone learns and grows at different speeds. Even that rate can be affected by a person's current mindset and emotional state. You have to give yourself time to process everything that's going on around you, especially everything that's going on inside of you. You have to be capable of giving yourself that same patience and understanding. Every decision won't be perfect, but be willing to make mistakes so you can become a better person. You are enough, and you have more than enough inside of you to find all of the wonderful things coming your way.

BROTHER, IT'S OKAY

How can anyone say a man isn't supposed to feel or have emotions? That's like saying a man isn't supposed to be human. Many men were taught that a man who expresses emotions, other than the manly ones, is soft. He isn't a real man because that's not what real men do. I don't care what gender you are, you feel just as much as the next human being. You may express those feelings differently, or you may try not to express them at all. Remember this, emotions may go unspoken, but they never go unexpressed. Everything that you feel will express itself in some way, at some point. It's no wonder that these real men who pretend they don't feel certain emotions end up having other destructive ways to express that emotion. Some internalize what they feel, choosing to lock it up inside of them. Soon, the stress of unexpressed emotions starts to cause pain and illnesses in the form of high blood pressure, ulcers, and a ton of other sicknesses. Some have such a difficult time processing their emotions that it comes out in the form of exhibiting abusive behavior to themselves and the people around them. It's time to break the cycle and bury the lie that men don't express their feelings. You can call it what you want, but I call it pain, hurt, and confusion. It's okay for a man to admit that he's hurt or in pain. It's okay. It's okay to admit that you don't have all of the answers. It's okay to admit that you need help. It's okay to not understand why you feel the way you feel. It's okay to shed tears. It's okay to have a broken heart. Brother, it's okay.

A DIFFERENT KINDA SPECIAL

This world won't always make sense. Sometimes, things just won't add up. Things won't always be fair. People won't always show you the respect you deserve. A person won't always consider your feelings before they do something. You won't always win. Some people will be better than you at certain tasks. You won't always be the fastest or the strongest. People will be smarter than you. You will fail and fall many times. Even after all that, there is no one who will ever be created quite like you. No one will ever have the combination of gifts and talents that you have. No one will ever be meant to accomplish what you were meant to do. No one will ever be capable of all of the things that you are capable of. You have a remarkably unique gift and purpose in the world. You are here for a very specific reason. It's a job that only you can do and only you were meant to do. Never take yourself, your purpose, and your potential for granted. You are a different kinda special!

THE DARKEST HOUR

You are not your pain. Pain doesn't define you. You define you. It won't always be easy, but know that pain is a valuable lesson needed for you to grow to the next level. In that hurt is an opportunity for you to dig deep and learn exactly who you are and what you want. Oh no, this is not the end for you. It's only the beginning. This is the beginning of something with the potential to be great. In your lowest time, you have the potential to rise to your highest peak. During your time of weakness, you will be made stronger than before. It may have temporarily held you back, but it underestimated just who you were. This minor setback will be the catalyst that slingshots you further than you ever thought possible. Your darkest hour will reveal the brightest light that will lead you to the best that's waiting for you.

RESPECT

Respect yourself by not continuously giving people the opportunity to disrespect you. People can only do as much as you allow them to do, and they can go only as far as you allow them to go. You deserve the same respect. You are worthy of it. Never let anyone treat you like you're less than. Know your worth.

FORGIVENESS FOR THE SPIRIT

To continue to relive the pain of the past is damaging to the spirit. To heal the spirit and practice forgiveness is the beginning of peace and happiness. There is no rest for the spirit that rewinds and replays the wrongs of the past. The mind that is haunted by feelings of unjust treatment will find it hard to rest. How can one truly find peace in their hearts if it is still injured from old wounds? Happiness will find it hard to make a home in a place that's filled with resentment. When one finds forgiveness, they pass through the darkness and find the light.

MIND YOUR HEART

Be conscious of the things that you hold in your heart because whatever is in your heart will create your life. The things you hold on the inside will eventually be reflected on the outside. Nothing remains unrevealed. That which is hidden can only remain hidden for a period of time. As seeds hide trees, flowers, and fruit, the state of your heart will precede the conditions of your life. Life is constantly unfolding from the inside out, and the thoughts in your heart will eventually reveal themselves in words and in actions. All that you are and all that you will become will be generated there. All that you will be and all that you will do must grow from what is planted in the soil of your heart. It is your responsibility to protect your heart and be mindful of your thoughts. If you neglect them, your heart and your mind will constantly be under attack and negatively influenced. Once you realize that your life in its totality is the sum total of your thoughts and values you place in your heart, you will discover the power that you possess to mold your own life.

DON'T BE DISCOURAGED

One of the most underrated enemies to success and happiness is discouragement. Discouragement hurts so much because it can cripple and demoralize. It paralyzes and keeps us from taking action. Discouragement can have us feeling sorry for ourselves and causes us to do nothing. Once we realize that this discouragement is self-inflicted, we have the power to change the whole situation around. In fact, the greatest enemy to discouragement is action. Taking intelligent action will empower you to get rid of discouragement, or it will try to get rid of you.

DID YOU LIVE TODAY?

Did you wake up with a fire in your soul and a desire to be your best self and pursue your dreams? Did you spend today living your truth and expressing your true voice? Did you spend the majority of your day doing meaningful activities, or was it wasted on distractions and useless activities? Did you have a genuine smile today? Did you make someone else smile? Did you have a good laugh? Did you tell the people you care about how much they mean to you? Did you do something today that filled you with joy? Did you help someone? Did you say thank you for all of your blessings? Did you do something spontaneous? Did you engage in an activity that you're passionate about? Did you meditate? Did you give yourself a moment to be present and just be? So, did you live today?

GREATNESS BELONGS

D on't allow life to be torn from you day by day. Don't go into each day being bombarded by distractions and forgetting what you really want from yourself and from your life. Don't say yes to things and end up with no time to do things that really matter to you. Greatness belongs to those who master their day. To those who subconsciously place themselves on a different level. They demand direction in their life. Their days have meaning, and they know that each day pushes them toward their destiny. It's as though they shoot an arrow of purpose as far as they can toward their goals each day and make it their mission to pick it up and shoot it forward again. They approach their daily struggles with focus, faith, and diligence. Even when they get lost, their presence of mind and sense of direction allows them to correct course. If they ever fall or despair, they possess the resilience to lift their heads, climb out of the hole, and continue their journey. They have a stunning commitment to their greater destiny. They have their own aim in life and wake up each day loyal to that cause with a blazing passion for it. Despite the struggles, they are relentless. They are always directing their intent, seeking opportunity, and always finding their way over and through any obstacles until they end up in the land of their dreams or laid in shadows of greatness for having died trying.

STRAGGLERS

Stragglers are always complaining, lack direction, have no passion, and refuse to put in the work it takes to get to where they want to be. They walk through life with no intention. Stragglers are easily distracted by the outside noise from the world and the inside noise in their head. They fail to look past what they are doing to see where they are headed. Stragglers have an illusion of productivity by checking off tasks on a list that has no definite aim. Stragglers are paralyzed by fear, content with laziness, and too influenced by the demands of others to chase their own dreams. They have no desire and lack discipline. Stragglers make excuse after excuse about why they can't accomplish something. They feel no responsibility to awaken their sleeping potential. Stragglers walk through life aimlessly, unable to face the truth that their life's agenda is absent of true purpose. The fullness of their lives and the completeness of their potential will never be realized because they did not stay true to all they were meant to be.

TRAPPED

Have you become so much like others that you are no longer yourself? Do you act like others to please and appease the people? If you are honest with yourself, do you feel like the people around you have no idea who you really are? Do you blindly follow other people's ideas even when they are not a reflection of what you truly believe? You shouldn't have to feel caged in your own skin. Your life is yours to form rather than conform. You don't have to cater to everyone else and be a pawn to the ideas and expectations of others, participating in a game that was never meant for you.

REFUSE

Refuse to suffer in silence. It settles in to weaken your power and poison your spirit. Never forget that speaking up for yourself is the fundamental practice of your freedom and living your truth.

AT THIS MOMENT

It only takes a moment to change your life. Not years, not months, not days. One moment. At this moment, you can determine where you want to be and decide not to quit until you get there. Anyone who has ever accomplished anything great can trace back the moment that put them on the path to their success. It could have been triggered by a personal reflection, a dream, a conversation, or even a hardship. It only takes a moment, but at that moment, you must exercise the greatest gift bestowed upon any human – free will. You always have a choice. Part of your power is recognizing that you have a choice. The other part is actually making it. Your life can literally change in a few months based on what you choose to do at this moment. You have to love yourself enough to choose the best that life has waiting for you, and you have to be brave enough to accept it.

FERTILE SOIL

You don't have to find happiness. Sometimes, you just have to make room for it. Sometimes, so much of your emotional space is taken up by the hurt that it leaves little room for happiness. It's almost impossible for happiness to blossom with that kind of foundation. Allow the pain to heal so you can have fertile soil for the happiness you deserve to grow.

QUANTIFIED SELF

We measure how many hours we work, how many hours we sleep, how much we weigh, how many degrees we have, how many calories we took in, and how many we burned. We have become more concerned with the number of followers and likes for attention, validation, and confirmation. We no longer foster genuine relationships with the people around us and have invested the majority of our time living as our digital selves in a false reality. We document just about every part of our day and all the moments in our lives. Yet, few of us know anything about ourselves. We are so consumed with keeping up with the task of being busy that we are not fully in touch with who we really are, how we really feel, and what we really want. Spend more time checking in with yourself and checking in with your soul. We live in an age where we are so busy documenting life that we don't take the time to actually experience it in all of its depth. We spend so much time checking in with the world that we check out from ourselves. Check in with yourself. Find reasons to proud of who you are and who you are becoming. Do things that make you happy, and find ways to contribute to the world. Be grateful for the day and all of its opportunities. This is how you check in with yourself, and these are the only measurements that truly matter.

CHOOSE YOURSELF

Give yourself permission to choose yourself. There's nothing selfish about giving yourself the opportunity to be happy, to be fulfilled, and to live the kind of life you deserve. You deserve to be in an environment that nourishes your dreams and builds your character, not one that tears you down and poisons your spirit. Choosing yourself is not only healthy, but it's also necessary. It sets the boundaries of what kind of energy you allow to occupy your space. It cultivates self-reliance and self-respect. To choose yourself doesn't mean you are neglecting the people you love, it means you are taking care of yourself, building yourself, and filling yourself so that you can give them the best of you.

I DECLARE

I declare that I will not let anyone tear me away from my dream. I declare that I won't allow the limits that other people place on their abilities be placed on me. I refuse to let people with small minds shrink my big vision. I won't sabotage my own potential with self-doubt. I refuse to believe less of myself, nor will I play the role of a victim in my life. My life is ultimately my choice.

HEART TO HEART

I want to listen to you so bad, but every time I listen to only you, we end up getting hurt. I mean – I appreciate your willingness to be open because I know you have so much love to give. I hear you loud and clear. I know you mean well, and I know you want the best for us, but we keep making the same mistakes over and over again. You tell me this time will be different, and I believe it. I want it just as bad as you do, so I let you lead. You can be so persuasive. Even when Mind is warning us not to do it again, he eventually gives in because he's tired of going back and forth with you. But that doesn't stop Mind from analyzing the situation, always looking for a reason for us to run, but you keep finding reasons for us to stay. No matter how bad the situation gets sometimes, you find a way to wake up with new hope. You hope beyond hope, almost blindly at times. That's what makes you so strong. Every time we get knocked down, you find a way to come through stronger than before. Even during those times when you feel broken to pieces, and you don't know how you're going to put yourself back together, you always find a way. For that, I am forever grateful. I know you can have your selfish moments, and you want what you want. Even when you know it's not the best for us, you love the rush it gives you at that moment. Usually, that rush is short-lived, and eventually, reality sets in. Then we are once again in the same place that we started. I don't blame you, but in order for us to get what we deserve, I can't just listen to you. We all have to work together because if we make decisions based on just what one of us wants, we will all suffer. The best things happen to us when we are in sync as much as possible. We know what we want, we know what fulfills us, and we know what makes us happy. What we want isn't a temporary fix, so we can't solve them with temporary solutions. We have to be patient with ourselves. We have to trust ourselves. We have to listen to each other's views. When we can do that in harmony, we tap into our true power, and we create a life that makes us feel the most alive.

THIS IS THE BEGINNING

This is not the end for you, this is just the beginning. This can be the start of something amazing, and it can start right now. Whatever you're going through ends today. Meaning, you are choosing that it ends, and you are putting things in motion to totally transform your circumstances and change your life forever. Your troubles can't, and will not, last. They are only temporary. You will not only get through this, but what started as a negative will be the very thing that triggers your breakthrough. You are taking your life off autopilot, and you are taking control of your own destiny. You are going to change the way you think and the way you talk to make sure that it is in alignment with what you really want. You will remain a hungry student, always willing to learn something new and apply it for even better results. You will replace old habits and instill new ones that strengthen your character and focus. You will decide that the only direction to go is forward and to never look back.

THE WATCHERS

Everyone is not meant to understand you. This vision you have for your life was given to you, and only you. So, they may never get why you are so passionate. They may never understand how someone could be so driven by a dream that they'll never be able to grasp. They may doubt that you will ever accomplish something that they can't see themselves, but that doesn't stop them from watching you try. With or without them, they watch you stumble your way through the journey, never being too proud to admit that you may not have it all figured out now but assured that you will. You may not see them, but they see you. You may never hear them, but they are listening. Many are waiting for you to fail, but eventually, they become intrigued by the relentlessness of the attempt. They soon become a part of the journey, whether they realize it or not. Those same people who have so much doubt become invested in a story they once believed to be fiction. They realize that this isn't just a dream for you, this your reality. No one can stop what is for you. It will be yours. What's yours is not for them to understand, but what's for you is yours for the taking.

TRUE LIGHT

I am beautiful by every definition of the word. Others don't have to see it or acknowledge it. I don't have to brag, boast, or convince anyone of how I feel about myself. True beauty shines regardless. It doesn't have to be touched or flipped on like a light switch. It radiates from the inside of me and warms every part of my body. This is my truth, and no one can take that from me. I may not have seen this remarkable piece of me before, but now, it's all I know. It's everything that I am. My light will no longer be subject to the blindness of those who can't see or live in the shadows of opinions of those who don't know. We can shine brighter together, or my shine can blind you to the reality. The choice is yours, but either way, I'm going to shine. Illuminating everything in my path so that those that come after me will be able see their way to their true selves. This is my true light, and it continues to reflect love back to my soul.

PEACE, BE STILL

Nothing speaks louder than silence. Life is loud, and the world inside is louder. Whatever is given out will then be reflected back. Only in silence can it be heard, and only in that space of nothingness can it be understood. The mind can speak to the heart, and the heart can resonate with the spirit. This is the native language of the universe, and it can now hear, understand, and manifest.

MY WORTH

My true worth cannot be quantified. It can't be found in a curve or a shape. My worth cannot be glorified in a size, a length, a color, or a tone. Hands can't touch my heart, and eyes can't see my soul. I am more than could ever be explored with any of the senses. My worth is carried in my mind through the glow in my spirit, and the shine in my smile.

THE POWER OF NO

Not knowing how to say no is where many lives decline into a place of stress and unhappiness. By constantly taking the role of the victim to the desires of others and neglecting their own. By becoming slaves to the agenda of others and being pressed by deadlines they didn't choose. By always waiting for instruction and direction from other people's lives. By being unable to rise to their own potential because they are so consumed with pleasing others. By being buried under the weight of other people's control and expectations. People will demand your time and attention, including people we love. Only when it is personally meaningful and advances us toward the life we want should the answer always be yes. So, beware of those who prey on those who have a desire to please. They will come again and again, as many times as they are allowed. These people don't consider what's important to you at that moment and can only see their own self-serving agenda. Learn to respectfully, but unapologetically, say no. No need to apologize for taking care of yourself. How we handle these enemies to our own progress will determine how effective we can actually be. Our progress will be doomed if it is filled with meaningless requests that drain us of what we need to accomplish to reach our own goals.

NEVER COMPROMISE

N ever compromise your dreams by repeating the lies of the weak, fearful, and uninspired. Your destiny is not for sale. To allow yourself to be less than you're capable of is to only exist and not to live.

SELF-OPPRESSION

No one wants to look in the mirror feeling like the person in the reflection is the cause of his or her frustrations. We want to see ourselves as masters of our own lives and creators of our own destinies. But sometimes, we take a look into our own tired eyes, and it's revealed that we are standing in our own way. Trying to motivate ourselves to be who we want to see looking back at us in the mirror can be difficult. There may be days when we are wrestling with our internal demons in an effort to break ourselves from their cold grip. Those demons make us stagnant and inactive toward things we really want. They keep us in a constant state of worry. These demons drain us of our vitality for life. We are always tired and lack energy. They weaken us to the point that we start to distrust our own abilities. No one is immune from fighting these demons at some point in their lives, but true enlightenment comes to those who are able to free themselves from all forms of self-oppression.

DEFEATING DOUBT

Doubt is a cunning beast that comes to rob, steal, and kill your dreams. Doubt is fed by pessimism. He tries to fill your head with recurring negative thoughts. The moment those doubting thoughts turn into words, he gets stronger. He begins to poison your mind with negative phrases and what ifs. His goal isn't to keep you from doing; his ultimate goal is to keep you from becoming. Becoming the person who you were always meant to be. It is only by faith that one can tear themselves from his clutches. We must choose to believe and hold on tightly to that belief, even in the face of the unknown. With faith, we gain the necessary strength to endure sadness, suffering, and loss, and know that they cannot last. It allows us to foster an unwavering belief in the capacity of our potential and our ability to succeed. If we can carry this kind of faith, doubt will surely be defeated. We must remember all the reasons we have to believe in ourselves. We have to remind ourselves of how far we've already come. No matter what, we have to find a reason to believe that tomorrow will be better, even in the midst of difficult days. In confirming these beliefs to ourselves, our Faith itself is strengthened. So, the next time doubt tries to creep in, replace it with the empowering thoughts of Faith. The more we choose Faith over doubt, the more we choose to follow our higher selves and exercise our divine power to weave the very fabric of our lives.

DELAYED BUT NOT DERAILED

S top letting procrastination delay your greatness. Procrastination will stop you from advancing toward your desired destination, poisoning you with crippling thoughts. Creating internal fears of hurt, pain, and rejection. Giving you the impression that you are not ready to make that decision. Making you believe that this is the best time and that you need to wait for the perfect time. Procrastination gives you false confidence in these negative thoughts as if it's just trying to protect you. If you have been waiting for the right time to start your business, tell the potential love of your life how you truly feel, take your career to the next level, take that dream vacation, or actually fight for what you truly want, procrastination is there. Procrastination is one of the greatest causes that have made potentially great men and women miss their moment. But there is still hope. The poison of procrastination can be defeated with action. When we decide to take action in the face of that fear, we activate a wave of power and possibility, freeing ourselves from procrastination's hold on our lives. The universe favors and rewards those who take decisive action. Therefore, that hope rests on the shoulders of whether or not action can override fear. So, let all of the excuses die. Let your actions push you through any hesitation.

In order to seize your destiny, you must do the things that you have been putting off and the things that you have feared the most. This strengthens your will, builds your confidence, and ensures your eventual success. Make a plan. Take action on advancing your life, regardless of fear and uncertainty. This is the stuff that legends are made of.

FERTILE SOIL

Make your mind and your spirit like fertile soil, so that the seeds you sow will be nourished and bring forth trees of fruitfulness. A closed mind and a hardened spirit are like hard, sunbaked clay that rejects any good seed attempting to find a place to be cultivated.

RECURRING DREAM

D o you have a dream that keeps coming to you? As if your mind is showing you a mental movie of a possible future? It was so vivid that you could see it plain as day. You could feel it as if you were already there. Then you came back to reality, just to be reminded that currently, your life looks nothing like what you saw in your vision. But no matter what your circumstances are, somehow, that picture, that vision keeps coming back. You try to force it out of your mind because the frustration of your current circumstances looking nothing like the life you envisioned. That dream that you keep having and that vision that you keep seeing isn't a mistake or an accident. It came to you for a reason, and you are the reason. It's not a preview of what can be; it's a preview of what should be. A vision of what's meant to be. Vision is the way God is communicating with your spirit to guide you toward your destiny. It's your potential future until you decide it is going to *be* your future.

THOUGHTS AND PURPOSE

W hat are thoughts without purpose but a sea of debris and wreckage drifting aimlessly?

CALMNESS

C almness is beautiful. Calmness is serene. Calmness precedes peace of heart and peace of mind. Only through the evolution of thought and understanding of self can it be created.

FULLNESS

Sometimes, we can miss the blessings around us, being lost in unawareness and missing the importance of this very moment, becoming dissatisfied with our current circumstances and attempting to live in the past or the distant future. Neither is possible. Tomorrow is gone, the future doesn't exist yet, so all you have is today. In order to harness the full power of today, we must bring our conscious mind fully into our present experience. We can't allow ourselves to get so conditioned by the daily grind of life that we become numb to the world around us. We must learn to feel again. We must set our intentions for what we want and who we want to become. Without awareness of our own energy and intention of purpose for what we desire, we cannot connect with others around us, nor with our higher life creating energy. In order to experience the fullness of today, we must meet life with our full presence in every moment.

DEMONS

Something inside is sabotaging your natural drive toward the things in life that make you feel purposed, feel happy, feel loved, and feel fulfilled. They scream for you to stop when you are pushed beyond your comfort zone. They try to scare you when you dare to be authentic and loving in this world. They attempt to burden you with personal obstacles when you seek to make a difference in the world around you. They try to poison you with worry and fear when they feel you are most vulnerable. Your life will be decided by how well you know them. Your destiny will be determined by how you defend yourself against them and how many battles you win against them each day of your life. With self-mastery, self-love, and self-understanding, we are slaves to the internal afflictions keeping us from living to our true potential. With a continuous and evolving sense of self, you will transcend any circumstance, free yourself from mental poverty, and claim the truest expression of your greatness.

SOUL FOOD

Even before we were, I was. Existing in the world beyond worlds, the space beyond time. Waiting to be placed into a special and unique vessel meant only for me. We were destined to find each other, and now, we are one. Every experience that you have is impressed on me. I am fed with everything from fear to pain to hate. Poison me with these, and I am weakened, injured, and no longer effective. In this state, I cannot protect us from the mental, emotional, and physical attacks that will surely come. I only hunger for energy that is aligned with the essence from which I was created. The energies of love, purpose, passion, and joy. This food strengthens me, nourishes me, energizes me, and empowers me to accomplish whatever is in alignment with our dominating thoughts. With this vibrancy, we can truly operate as we were intended. We will no longer be victims but victors. Though we will face obstacles, we are heavily equipped with the weapons that can surely defeat any enemy that comes against us, inside and out.

ACQUAINTANCES

Just because you don't consider them friends, it doesn't mean that they don't have an affect on you. The people you call acquaintances can have just as much of an impact on your life. Some have no ill intentions, but some can transfer their negativity on your life just as easily. Constant gossiping, complaining, and a bad attitude can rub off on your day and your life. Understand that everyone is energy, no matter how much or how long you expose yourself to them. Of course, if you're around people you consider friends more, you are more likely to be influenced by them, but it only takes one encounter with an acquaintance to make an impact. You are actually more likely to react negatively toward something they might say or do. Since you don't consider them your friend, they're less likely to get a pass. So, at the end of the day, it's more about how you have built your own character and values and less about other people. When you understand yourself and what's really important, you will more than likely respond in a positive way, regardless of the person and the circumstances. So, be mindful of the people and energy you come in contact with. We are all energy. Be intentional with the energy you put out, and be protective of the energy you allow in, especially if it isn't in alignment with yours.

SELF-COMPASSION

You're not going to be your strongest in every situation. You're not going to be your bravest in meeting every obstacle. You don't have to always feel whole to be loved completely. It's not just you. You are not alone. Give yourself permission to not only have compassion but to be able to give compassion to yourself. You are doing the best you can. You deserve it.

PLANTED IN FAITH

Don't dig up in doubt what you planted in Faith. How many times have you asked or prayed for something, but soon after, you start coming up with all the what ifs you can think of?

One minute, you're full of positive energy, the next minute, you're dropping excuse after excuse about what you don't have, what you don't know, and how you're going to do it.

I know...it's hard when you want something so bad, and you don't see anything changing, or the same things keep happening. That's so frustrating! But the one thing you do know is that when you start doubting yourself, you're not helping the situation at all. You know you're making yourself feel worse, but you allow yourself to stay in that space. If you say you want it, want it! If you say you can do it, do it! If you say you're a believer, believe! Don't believe with what you say about it, believe with what you DO ABOUT IT!

110%

No one has ever become great by merely dabbling in something. If you really want it, you have to immerse yourself in it. You have to work to master it. You have to learn as much about it as you can. You're going to have to try out some different things, allowing yourself to fail in order to learn and grow. So, don't do it a little. If you're going to do it, do it big, and give it 110%.

AT PEACE

One day, you wake up, and you're in this place. You're in this place where everything feels right. Your heart is calm. Your soul is on fire. Your thoughts are positive. Your vision is clear. You're at peace. You're at peace with where you've been, at peace with what you've been through, and at peace with where you're going.

FINDING YOURSELF

Y ou don't always need outside motivation or someone around in order to find yourself. Wherever you're trying to go and whatever you're trying to accomplish, it's an inside job. Having support is good, but at the end of the day, no one can do it for you. No one can want it for you. You have to want it bad enough for yourself. Bad enough that you are willing to do the work on yourself by yourself.

GO THROUGH IT

There comes a time when you have to let go of everything that's not contributing to your success, your happiness, or your growth. When you have to stop fighting a life you've outgrown, and trust that everything will work out, even you can't see how right now. At first, things may feel messy and difficult, and you may feel scared and lost. Embrace the journey. The darkness of change leads to the light of possibility, but first, you have to go through it.

SOMETHING SPECIAL

When people used to tell me that there was something special about me, I would always reply that *I'm nothing special.* When people would say that I was so different from anyone they had ever met, I would tell them that *I am just like everyone else.* One day, a woman told me that I had a special gift that would be a blessing to others. When I tried to tell her, *I was just a normal guy,* she abruptly stopped me. She said she knew I was being humble, but that I should never diminish the power of my gift and my purpose. She reminded me that you are, indeed, something special. You are special for everything that you were, everything that you are, and everything that you will become. There is no one that has been through exactly what you have been through. You have a unique perspective of this life that no one else has. You have a collection of gifts, talents, and experiences that make you more special than you could ever imagine. There is no person that can ever be compared to you. It doesn't matter what they look like, what they have, or who they are, they are not you and never can be. Take pride in that. To understand your uniqueness is to be in possession of your true power, which creates breakthroughs. There is no selfishness in recognizing this power. Only when it's abused or used to make someone else feel inferior is it turned to darkness. But, when this self-mastery is cultivated, it can be a beacon of light. Recognizing this power doesn't diminish your humility, it raises it to a new level. It's a blessing to be you. Yes, any life of self-exploration comes with obstacles and challenges, but these are needed in order to grow and gain vital experience. These stories become your test. These tests become your testimony. You have so much potential. You have an important purpose that only you can fulfill. There is something this world needs that only you can provide. In the meantime, don't forget to love and honor yourself because you are something special.

STOP WAITING

Stop waiting to find out who you are. Stop waiting to declare your dreams. You will struggle for what you want until you are able to open yourself up fully to love and life. Stop waiting for a sudden boost of confidence and courage to take action. Stop waiting for someone to give you permission to activate your potential. Courage is a choice, and that permission to move forward in boldness can only be self-granted. Seeking change is a journey filled with internal demons, self-inflicted wounds, and miles of personal growth opportunities. Stop waiting for the perfect conditions, and take the first steps. Remember, who you ultimately become is not the sum total of your intentions, but rather, the sum total of your actions. Those who choose to take the initiative to seize their own destiny can rise and soar to heights of their true greatness. Don't hesitate or take this moment for granted. This moment is begging for you to begin something that can be the defining moment of the rest of your life.

SICK AND TIRED

We get exhausted. Life has a way of taking a toll on us. It can beat us down psychologically, emotionally, and physically until we resemble only a shell of our former selves. Even the conversations around us echo the existence of sick and tired people. The emotional energy of the world can weigh so heavy that we feel we are holding ourselves up with everything we have left. So many are sacrificing their own well-being and peace in the chase for riches and success. We have become cold. Cold on the inside and cold toward each other. Where is the energy? Where is the laughter? Where did the passion for a fully engaged life go? How can we reignite the fire inside of us that made us feel the most alive? Right now, the ultimate duty in our lives is to rekindle that magic. To release ourselves from the false imprisonment of past mistakes and pain. To step out of the comfort of a mundane, robotic existence and explore new adventures. To break away from the illusions of perceived success and happiness and get in touch with what speaks to our souls once again.

SACRIFICES

You don't have to compromise who you are and what you want when life becomes difficult. You don't have to sacrifice your individuality and integrity for success. When things don't go the way you want them to, you don't have to create a habit of quitting or giving up too soon. You don't have to give up what you truly believe in for the sake of a false sense of popularity. Even in times of struggle and desperation, you should never have to compromise who you are. In those moments, you must not follow the impulse to be weak. You must be strong and courageous in the midst of your troubles. Your love of self and commitment to your integrity must be in line with your highest values. To compromise who you are may bring about temporary happiness and success, but it will not last. True victory belongs to those who remain true to themselves despite the temptation to sacrifice who they truly are.

MADE FOR LOVE

We may get to a point in our lives when we feel like we can no longer give the kind of love we want or receive the kind of love we need. We began to feel like love itself has become our enemy. With each potentially meaningful interaction, we start filtering love rather than feeling it. When we were hurt, we felt like our capability to love was damaged. But the truth is, hurt has nothing to do with love, and love is unaffected by pain. Love is a powerful spirit of divine proportions. Love is omnipresent, abundant, and free. It is the energy that is flowing throughout everyone and everything. At times, it may feel like it's gone, but love is never absent from our lives. Love can't be confined to hearts or bound by relationships. Love is a free spirit, so it can't be owned. Love is ever-present, so it can't be lost. When we become aware of our own ability to recognize love and harness it within ourselves at any given time, love can never diminish. So, if we allow love to die, we become the cause of our own suffering. We must realize that freeing ourselves from past pain and opening up to love again gives us access to our true strength. To stand before the world and give love without fear of hurt or looking for it in return. This is the ultimate act of courage.

THE FEW

What happened to ideals, virtue, and humanity? Too many people remain silent and don't call out wrongs when they see it. This has created the reemergence of a global failure in leadership, which has birthed an increase in poverty and greed. People are afraid to demand more from their leaders. The moral fiber of humility and understanding that we were attempting to weave has been disassembled thread by thread. From these moments of darkness and uncertainty will arise a chosen few. The few who are unafraid to challenge the status quo. The few who seek higher truths with every fiber of their being. The few who are built on morals and values. The few who are driven and motivated by compassion. The few who are inspired by history, with the hope to not repeat it, but to make it.

PRESENCE

Take a moment to stop, be still, breathe, and feel. Sense the stillness of the atmosphere, the fullness of presence, the beauty of life, and the perfection of the moment. Storming through life, neglecting the senses and surroundings, causes blindness to truth and deafness to understanding. The magic of potential lives in this very moment. Being numbed by pain and stressing through life only leads to the true spirit and essence of the person being stripped from the Now. All that is left is a shell and an unrecognizable reflection. The cost is catastrophic and results in creating an unexperienced life; a life filled with blurred moments and moments not fully lived. Slow down to fully experience this singular moment and all of its worth. Stretch the moment so you can truly sense its depth. Your life experience is meant to be vibrant, deeply felt, and full of meaningful moments. This day - this moment - is to be lived, experienced, and appreciated for all it is and all that it can possibly be.

MORE POWER

No longer will we allow ourselves to become a victim of self-imposed struggle. We must not undervalue our potential by looking down or aiming low. We will not let our will fade or our efforts be dampened by distraction and criticism. We must choose not to let negative energy invade our minds, fill our hearts with anger, or fill our mouths with complaints. No longer will we be ruled by the undisciplined part of ourselves searching for comfort, convenience, and ease. The limits that smaller thinking individuals place on their lives won't poison our potential. We will no longer strive for the support and validation of those who are deaf to our true voices. Those who are in alignment with our spirit and our purpose will find us as a kindred spirit that will stand behind us, and they will stand with us. No longer can we let the giant inside us sleep. We must awaken and realize there is greatness awaiting within us and for us. There is more energy. There is more power. There is more love. There is more life. We will not wait for change to come into our lives. The change will not come to us, rather, the change will come from within us and from us. We won't hope for change by mere chance, we will call upon the courage to change it ourselves. Despite all the obstacles that stand in our way, we know and believe that our dreams are worth the struggle. In the name of our destiny, we exercise our true strength to live our dreams, find our peace, and strive for greatness.

INFLUENCER

We can gain insight and perspective from others, but we are the most influential forces in shaping our lives. Our circumstances are not cemented in the present; therefore, they are not permanent. Our potential is not dead, only buried under fear, doubt, and lack of action. We are the architects of our lives with the ability to bend reality to our dreams and craft the lives we desire. We can no longer afford to wait for permission or a perfect time any longer. Our struggle doesn't define us but within it, we accomplish the growth necessary to change our lives and recreate ourselves. We must remind ourselves that everything that we need is accessible and readily available inside of us now. Along with the vision that was revealed to you was the ability to make it a reality built inside of you. Everything that we need to start is living within us.

SELF-GOVERNED SOUL

No matter the circumstances, your life eventually becomes a reflection of your own state of consciousness. Everything that you know must pass through the gateway of experience, and as such, becomes a part of yourself. Your subconscious can't distinguish between thoughts of desire and joy or those of sorrow and pain. So, by your own thoughts, you create your life, your world, and your universe. As you build yourself from within by the power of your thoughts, your life and circumstances shape themselves accordingly. Whatever is in your innermost heart will sooner or later reveal itself in your life. Every soul attracts what hums to the same vibration. What you attract will be drawn by the quality and power it puts into the universe. Every soul is a complex combination of experiences and thoughts, and the physical body is the vehicle in which these things are manifested. Whether you are fearful or fearless, within the soul lies its own state of being. Only when you're not in the understanding of this will you be thrown off course or distracted when life happens. When you know the truth of the source of your strength and power, you will be able to weather those storms and overcome those obstacles. Any troubles or setbacks become minor and temporary. When you begin to realize this, you will begin to control your thoughts and discipline your mind, eliminating all thoughts that are not in line with your true desires. Your inner being becomes a beacon of joy, compassion, strength, beauty, and love. Even in the midst of pain and ugliness, you will be able to see beauty. Where your weaker mind once saw disaster and confusion, your stronger mind now sees perfection in the making. You will then be the god of your inner world, passing from revelation to realization, discovering the power of a self-governed soul.

MASTER OF SOUL

To fear or worry is to curse that which you truly desire. How can one fear if one truly believes in the Eternal, the Omnipotent, and the Boundless? It is in this state of mind that all weakness and failure thrive, for they represent the disintegration of the positive forces which are at the source of their power. To overcome these negative conditions of the mind is to enter into a life of power. It is to cease to be a slave of circumstance, mediocrity, and mental poverty and to become the master of your own destiny. This can only be accomplished with a persistent growth of internal knowledge. To deny the existence of negative thoughts is not realistic, but with daily mental practice, those thoughts can be transcended and risen above. To only think positive will not suffice or change the circumstances. You must ingrain yourself with an unwavering belief in self, along with right and swift action. The journey of self-mastery quickly leads to a knowledge of one's internal forces, which eventually leads to the acquisition of power that can be directed toward one's aim. The measure in which you are able to master yourself will be the measure in which you are able to master your outward circumstances. You are in control of your mind and your energy instead of being controlled by them. There is nothing that strong Faith and certainty of purpose can't accomplish. Be guided absolutely and entirely by your vision and not by the shadows of fear. There is no vision that can't be actualized by the intelligent use and direction of one's soul force. Every thought you think is a force sent out, and it will go out to seek energy that is in like vibration with it. As you succeed in gaining mastery over your energy and thoughts, you will begin to feel the silent power growing inside of you. As you rise above the destructive thoughts, you will come in contact with the kind of joy, strength, and power that are only accessible through self-mastery. The one who succeeds in understanding the divinity in this power realizes that all the forces of the universe will move and realign for one who is the master of his/her soul.

SELFLESS LOVE

Deep in every human heart is the spirit of divine love, whose essence is undying and eternal. This love is permanent and imperishable. The highest righteousness is to live in it and become fully conscious of it. To become one with Truth, one with God, and one with the heart of all things and to know our own divine nature. To reach this love, one must learn to be of steady heart and calm mind. To understand and experience it, one must be at peace with self and of strong faith. Those who strive for it must understand that they will be met with many necessary obstacles designed to help them gain real wisdom. Experience will be the teacher, and the lessons will be the guide.

The higher-self understands that there is no such thing as defeat. Failure is real, but not reality. With every slip comes knowledge, and with every fall comes strength. This valuable experience gained becomes a vein in which wisdom can be extracted and become the life's blood flowing toward what it was sent out to accomplish. This selfless love will then be revealed to you. It will awaken within you, drawing you closer to the eternal heart. This kind of love embraces the whole universe and contains within itself the whole. No pain can come from a love that is so absolutely pure that it seeks nothing for itself. Selfless love draws the soul and knows no sorrow. It is the place where a broken heart can find shelter from the rain, hurt, and pain, and find rest, peace, and comfort. This love seeks no rewards and leaves behind no heartaches. This is a love beyond the reach of self. When the heart and mind are emptied of self, only then can you find selfless love. To realize selfless love is to become new. It is a state of knowledge that destroys past transgressions and lifts the soul into a realization of divine peace and tranquility. To know this love is to be at the heart of all things and realize its true power. It can't be attained by trying to gain victory over the world, but by gaining victory over self. Train your mind in gentleness. Train your heart in compassion. Train your mouth in stillness. To know that love is universal and to be free. This is peace. This is joy. This is the realization of selfless love.

WHAT YOU SEE IS WHAT YOU GET

You aren't who you think you are. You are who you believe you are. What do you see when you look in the mirror? Who do you see when you look past the physical exterior? The self-image that you hold in your heart, positive or negative, will become your truth. Your truth will attract like energy. Your truth will produce like-life experiences. Never attempt to paint an image of yourself on someone else's canvas. Any perception of you that doesn't come from your Creator is inaccurate and inauthentic. The Originator is the only artist that could ever capture the full expression of your truth and true potential. You are so much more. They will try to place you in boxes that you could never fit in and make you put on masks that you were never meant to wear. The very things that will make you great will be the very thing they will try to get you to change. You were created as an ideal, so they have no idea. Know yourself. Know your power. Know your truth. Never diminish the fullness of your personality for the comfort of those who are blind to its beauty. They have no intention of understanding, and they were never meant to. Be you. All of you in all of its splendor. How they feel about you is not your business, but how you feel about you is the brush that will paint your reality. Whether you choose to paint it with muted strokes of blacks and grays or vibrant splashes of blues and greens is up to you. You are the artist of your life. You were never meant to live in pieces, as you were already created as a masterpiece.

STRANGER DANGER

You are not obligated to open up your world to strangers. Everyone that is interested in your business is not always there for your best interest. Some come to be spectators, and some come to sabotage. Others will come with selfish aims, with only intentions to be takers and not givers. You don't owe them anything, but you owe yourself everything. Your energy is your life. Anyone that doesn't add any value to who you are or who you want to become doesn't belong in your world. You shouldn't feel bad about it. If you want success, happiness, and peace, it's critical that you value your energy and who you choose to invest your time in. It's nothing personal, it's your life.

COMPLETE

No other person can ever define you or complete you. You should never feel like you need someone else to be whole. Remember, you are still you without them.

BELIEVE

Believe that you deserve the life you want now. Believe that you deserve to be happy now. Believe that you deserve to be loved now. No one can believe this for you. You have to believe it for yourself. You have to believe in yourself. You have to want it for yourself. No one can want it for you.

IN CONTROL

You have to come to terms with the things that happened in your life that you couldn't control. There may have been people you cared about who did you wrong for no good reason. It hurt, and maybe it still does, but that's not the end of your story. You can't blame yourself for other people's decisions. You can't even blame yourself for the bad decisions you may have made in the past. That was you then, but that doesn't mean that it's you now. In fact, those are the same choices that help shape the person you are today. So, stop beating yourself up when things happen that are beyond your control. Don't take it so personally when people you care about put themselves in bad circumstances based on their choices. It's okay to empathize, but don't make their mistakes your own.

TRUST

Trust is powerful. Trust is weak. Trust is foundational. Trust is fragile. Trust is belief. Trust is doubt. Trust is confidence. Trust is fear. Trust is knowledge. Trust is ignorance. Trust is hope. Trust is hopelessness Trust is love. Trust is pain.

ON DEMAND

Create dreams and goals that will demand nothing less than the best that you are capable of. The mind seeks stimulation, the heart yearns for growth, and the body is compelled by action. Be courageous enough to take the first steps without knowing what the next will be.

STORMY WEATHER

We have moments when we don't feel good about ourselves. At times, we may not like ourselves and maybe even not love ourselves. In those times, we must look to the ones who care about us the most. We must borrow their perspective and look through their eyes to see what they see in you. Through their eyes, they see love. In their eyes, they see everything that is beautiful. They see the best in us even when we're at our worst. When we've made mistakes in the past, they see who we are, rather than who we were. Let them be our rock during stormy weather. When we fall down, we must grab a hold of their hand, and allow them to lift us up. Even when we feel we deserve nothing, they are prepared to give us everything. Where we see bad, they see good. We can't allow ourselves to be too proud to lean on those who love us when we feel too weak to stand on our own.

LEAP

Jump into the ocean of your dreams. Don't overwhelm yourself with every detail and every question. Everything that you need will be provided, and each step will be revealed. But first, you must take the leap. Don't be the person to find something wrong at every turn, only to use it as an excuse not to go forward or to turn around. Action is the wave ridden by all those who have achieved extraordinary feats and found greatness. They are not stuck in a cycle of contemplation and waiting for perfect conditions. Those who wait are left at the shore to watch the exhilarating adventure of those who chose to claim their own destiny.

SELF-TALK

In this lifetime, you will never have more conversations with anyone more than with yourself. In a sense, you have to be your own best friend. You have to be able to be honest with yourself. When there's no one around, you have to become your own source of inspiration and motivation. You have to believe in you when nobody else does. You have to be the one who is speaking life into your dreams. You must never think less of yourself. You must never talk down to yourself. It was written that a house divided against itself cannot stand. It is up to you, and no one else, to complete you. At times, it will feel like you don't know what to say to yourself. You will struggle, and in your moments of weakness, you will find it hard to find thoughts or words. That's when you must be able to dig deep into yourself to find those conversations when you promised that you wouldn't give up on yourself. Those times when you said you believed in yourself. Remember the times when you kept going because you truly believed that your purpose was bigger than your pain. So, every day, your self-talk should be about strength, happiness, and passion. The conversation should be so vivid that it imprints images and visions that you can see clearly in your mind.

You should be able to feel it as if it was already your reality because it is. All you have to do is decide.

THE TRUTH

I know what it's like to feel like giving up. To feel like you have given everything that you have and everything that you are to something, but that something doesn't give it back to you in return. I know what it's like to feel useless. To feel like no matter how much you try to do, it's never enough. I know what it's like to be confused by this life. To feel like everything that you've believed in may have been a lie. I know what it's like to not love yourself. To feel like your life doesn't have the value and meaning that it should. I know what it's like to be sick and tired. To feel like you've gone through so much pain that you feel empty inside. But knowing all of that is the very thing that led me to this truth. The truth that nothing about me is a mistake. Everything that I've gone through was only meant to prepare me for who I was meant to become. The truth that I have a unique purpose in this world. There are things that the world needs that I, and I alone, can accomplish. The truth that I am Spirit and a force of nature. The energy that created the earth, formed the universe, and birthed life flows in me and through me. The truth that I am love. I was made of love and from love, so in myself, I am love. I can never lose myself. The truth that I was given free will. I alone am responsible for my life. I must become the energy of happiness, love, and prosperity that I want to attract into my own life. And that's the truth!

THE BOLD

Those who fail to take action and take control of their own lives rely too heavily on others for their success, happiness, and care. Their mental maturity level is still that of a child waiting for their mom or dad to give them a nod of approval or permission. They are looking to others to be their cheerleaders and approve their actions. If they don't receive that permission, they fail to take any action. They make no significant progress in life due to being trapped by a fear of failure, criticism, and abandonment. They become lifetime followers, never allowing themselves to be the one to make the footprints for others to follow. You don't need permission from the world. Anything or anyone that has ever become great was once the most heavily criticized. You must be strong. You must be fearless. You must be bold. The bold never limit their vision based on the inability of others to see it or understand it. The bold will start a task without anyone else's feedback or permission. The bold doesn't wait for others to move; the bold are movers. Society only gives permission to be normal and conform to traditions. They will never grant permission to think freely, question dated ideals, and be individuals. Being bold isn't easy. Being bold will sometimes require going against cultural traditions, family values, and loved ones. Sometimes, even the people you care about the most won't understand and support your decisions. You will come against heavy resistance in pushing against conditioned beliefs that don't fit that box. This is the reality of the bold that must be faced for all those who seek to realize their dreams, their potential, and their truth. This decision will ultimately decide the level of fulfillment and sense of satisfaction that you will get from this life. One of the greatest permissions ever granted to you by God was the permission to follow your heart.

PRAYED OUT

I'm so tired. My body is tired, my mind is tired, my spirit is tired. I've been praying so hard for so long, I'm not so sure anybody is listening anymore. Years of reading, long days of studying, and late nights of meditating. And nothing… I give and give and give, and I don't know if I have anything left to give. I have believed with every fiber of my being, I have remained steadfast in the middle of every storm, and I have dedicated everything that I am and everything that I will become to an ideal. I've prayed for strength, and yet I'm weary. I've prayed for understanding that has been met with painful silence. I've prayed for change, yet I remain in this sunken place. Have I been living a lie? Is everything that I have believed and dedicated my life to true? I don't even know anymore. I don't know which way I'm going or which way to turn. I keep pouring out my heart, hoping to be filled, but I still feel empty and confused. Yet I go back to the Word to feed my spirit, and still, I remain weak and running out of strength to fight. At times, I just feel like crying out, but I have no more tears left to cry. Each day, I keep living this nightmare over and over again. Every day, I put on the mask to hide the pain behind it. Even in midst of that pain, there is always a glimmer of hope. This is it! Today, something is going to happen that will change everything. This is the day that all of the hard work, all of the sacrifice, all of the praying, all of the meditating, all of the positive thinking, all of the failures, and all of the madness will make sense. I wait patiently and optimistically. Days go by, then weeks go by, then months go by, and then years go by. Nothing. Nothing but more pain and more disappointment. Then, I get into the space of impenetrable frustration when I don't even want to take any of the advice that I would give someone else. I don't want to hear how it's going to be alright. Don't tell me to think positive. Don't tell me to keep praying. Don't feel sorry for me. I don't want to talk. I don't want a hug. Just...let me be. After all of that. After all, I've been through. The pain, the hurt, the frustration, the disappointment, and the losses...I still believe! I still believe that God loves me, He is here with me, and He has a plan for me. I still believe that I am meant for something great, and the vision for my life is still true. I still believe in my potential and my purpose. I still believe in myself. I still believe in prayer. I have come too far to quit now. There are people who have poured into me, who believe in me and love me, who I don't want to let down. Most of all, I don't want to let myself down. I am favored, and I am blessed. I am grateful for my struggle because it made me into who I am and who I am becoming. I am grateful for what I have because as hard as I think I have it, there are people who have it much worse. I am grateful for each breath and each day. Each day is a blessing. Each day is an opportunity. Each day in itself is a reason to be happy and find more happiness inside. I know that more obstacles will come to try to trip me up. More storms will arise to try and rain down on me. I may stumble, but I will keep moving forward. I may fall, but I will get back up each and every time. I will keep the Faith. I will stay strong. I will stay on the path. I will keep pushing. I will keep believing. I keep praying.

NEVER ENOUGH

There isn't enough is the cry of those who are still blind to the abundance of the universe. They have failed to come to the realization that all of the resources they will ever need comes from within. The only way we can acquire the knowledge we need to succeed is to be willing to take the action. From those actions, we gain the valuable experience needed to navigate our way to our desired destination. Time isn't our problem. It's not that we need more time, we just need a *why* strong enough push us to use the time that we have more effectively. We will only receive the level that we are willing to rise to. Those who succeed aren't reacting to life, they are consistently acting on the life that they want to create. So, when the moment comes to meet them, as it most certainly will, they remain prepared and ready to take full advantage of it. All that we need is abundantly within, and all that is attracted to us is in accordance with our own vision, resilience, and resourcefulness.

THE SOFTEST PLACE ON EARTH

There is no place like your heart. Your heart is the bridge between the natural and the spiritual world. Its ability to feel from both worlds simultaneously makes it the strongest and most sensitive part of you. So, protect your heart. Listen to it. Feel it as yourself. Sometimes, to neglect the heart is to neglect the self, but sometimes to neglect the self is to protect the heart.

Utilize its strength, but respect its gentleness. Your heart is the beacon that attracts your dreams to you. It also warns you if the energy around you isn't aligned with its deepest needs. Don't allow your heart to be the victim. Let it be your strength, your protector, and your connection to the spiritual world where all that will ever be exists.

THE STRUGGLE IS REAL

There is no significant advancement that can be accomplished in life without struggle. Coming to terms with this early on gives you the ability to anticipate it and prepare for it. Struggle is the consequence of higher ambition and is necessary for advancement. It is the sacrifice made to better ourselves, prove ourselves, and realize who we truly are. Struggle reveals the depth of the effort. It reveals how much we are willing to give of ourselves to accomplish that which we say we desire. The power to command our destiny comes from our willingness to struggle through effort, learning, and growth. Don't fear the hardships of facing your limitations and trying new things. Real progress, real success, and real change requires real effort. We must not get too comfortable or fall into complacency. We must focus on continually advancing our lives if we want to reach our true potential. The only language our goals and desires respond to is action.

I KNOW

I Know that there is a life of abundance inside of me. I know that all that I am and all that I will become is enough. I know that I am complete within, and I am complete without. I know that I am responsible for my own joy. I know that my past doesn't define me, but it taught me. I know that I am ultimately responsible for my needs. I know that I am not perfect, but I can give a perfect effort. I know that I am worthy and worth it. I know that I am allowed to make mistakes and grow from them. I know that I am thriving even in moments of failure. I know that my success, my happiness, my greatness, and my life is my decision.

BROKENNESS

A wise woman said that "healing is helping to learn new ways to love myself through pain. That you're not broken, you're becoming." Learning through hurt isn't an easy or fun process. It hurts. It hurts so much that there are no words to describe it, you can only feel it. Sometimes, the weight of carrying the pain on the journey to healing is harder than the pain itself. Having to feel it over and over again, reliving it each day, takes a toll on a person's body, mind, heart, and spirit. What brokenness does is puts our soul in a state of openness and vulnerability. You not only find yourself, you also discover what your truth really is. You are being rebuilt from the ground up. You are being strengthened from the inside out. You are being born again in the image of your true needs. You learn the importance of self-forgiveness, self-understanding, and self-care. You are not broken, you are repairing. You are not in pieces, you are being made whole. You are not failing, you are becoming.

GREATER

Destiny smiles at those whose actions and thoughts are in alignment with their values and priorities in life. Our greater self becomes the driving force behind our behavior and character. The greater good becomes the fabric woven with threads of love, humility, and peace to be placed over the coldness of the world. We must define the best of who we are. We must decide what we will stand for. We must claim the life that is rightfully ours. The life predestined before the beginning of time.

SACRED SPACE

B e mindful about who you expose yourself and your energy to. Everyone that comes into your space doesn't always have your best interest at heart. When you hunger for more from your life, and you continue to feed yourself with the positive energy that you need, they are starving. They will try to project their own doubts and limitations on you and your life. If you are not mentally strong or spiritually sound, that negative energy can be really damaging to you and everything around you. Energy is a spirit. There's only so much negative energy you can take before it starts to attach itself to you. It may start with rising thoughts of doubt and poison in your mind. That poison then spreads throughout your body and begins to affect your attitude and your mood. Eventually, the same toxic energy starts to come out of your mouth in how you speak to others and how you talk to yourself. Where there once was a soul filled with optimism, excitement, and vibrant energy, now the soul houses a spirit filled with doubt, fear, and pessimism. Be cautious of the company you keep and the environments you reside in. Make sure that the people and spaces that you are blessing with your presence are radiating positive energy. Do you feel happier when you are around them? Do you feel inspired and motivated?

Preserve your light for places that nurture your luminance. Be around people who can not only handle your shine but want it to be brighter. There will be those who see your glow from a distance, and they become a shade in an attempt to dim your light. There will also be those who treat you like an outlet, who only want to plug into you and drain you. Your space is sacred. Your space is precious. Your space isn't meant for everyone, but for those who have proven they respect and appreciate it. For those special souls who want nothing from you, but they want everything for you.

DISAPPOINTMENT

D o not fear disappointment. Those who say they don't get disappointed have chosen to live below their real dreams and their true desires. Those who have not tasted the bitterness of disappointment have not experienced anything new or significant. Those people have found comfort in mediocrity. For those who do try, the problem is not in being disappointed itself, the problem is the reaction to the disappointment. You can choose to quit in an attempt to spare yourself from further hurt, only to learn that this choice will become the death of your dreams and the fulfilled life that you desire. You can try to use disappointment as an excuse or a justification for quitting. You will blend into the crowd of the nameless and faceless in an attempt to have a life of ease and ignore the fulfilling work needed to have a life of achievement. Or you can choose to use disappointment as tools of experience that gives you valuable insight that you could not have gained anywhere else. Those people understand that disappointment is the reality of those who aim for greatness in every field of human endeavor. These inspiring individuals realize that disappointment is necessary and holds no power over them, but it, in fact, empowers them. Soon, with a learning mindset, disappointment dies and transforms into opportunities to learn and understand how to be better and better each time. So, don't break your commitments to yourself, to your dreams, and to all the things that are important to you. Don't let disappointment grow into an identity of failure. Be one of the extraordinary people who, when they feel disappointment, learn from it, let it go, and move on. They allow disappointment to increase their competency, not to define their character.

INTROVERT

I used to think that keeping to myself meant that I was too shy or being antisocial. As I got older, I learned that I enjoy being alone because I really like being at peace. It was only being in environments that weren't aligned with my values, priorities, and goals that made me uncomfortable. So, it turns out, I was actually extremely outgoing when I was around people who were uplifting, passionate, happy, and peaceful.

NO APOLOGIES NECESSARY

You are not obligated to remain the same person you were a year ago, a week ago, or even five minutes ago. You have the right to grow. You have permission to improve your circumstances. You have the right to better yourself. You have the right to want more from your life and for your life. No apologies necessary.

BEHIND CLOSED DOORS

You never know what someone is dealing with behind closed doors. No matter how happy they look, no matter how big they smile, no matter how much they laugh, they can be going through hell inside. We have no idea what people have had to experience and go through in their past. We don't even know what they may be dealing with in their present. So, be kind to others, even when you have nothing to gain from it. You never know whose day you are impacting in a positive way. One act of kindness, one display of compassion can give someone the hope they need to make it through. You may not only be making their day, you could also be changing their lives.

NO EXPLANATION NEEDED

Make sure you always make yourself and your well-being a priority. At the end of the day, it is your responsibility. You don't owe anyone an explanation for taking care of yourself.

DESPERATE MEASURES

We have all made hasty and bad decisions in moments of desperation. When we feel like we don't have a choice, in order to take care of ourselves or our loved ones, we do things that go against what we truly believe. Desperation can make a moral person break their integrity. In the name of a quick dollar, we can stoop to the most egregious levels of dishonesty. We will compromise ourselves and our own values in the most desperate times that we feel calls for desperate measures. Desperation causes the hungry to steal, the weak to prey, and the just to cheat. Even in the most desperate moments, we must choose not to compromise who we are. We must decide to stand for the morals and the values that are near and dear to our hearts. The best of us will be faced with moments when we are desperate and afraid, and the way we respond in that moment will reveal who we are as a person. When our hour arrives, let us respond based on our highest values and our highest self and show just what we're made of.

THE MOST BEAUTIFUL THING IN THE WORLD

There is no beauty in the world more perfect than unashamed, unfiltered, and unconditional love. We are at our best as humans when we live in love. Living in love is how we were designed to be. When we try to deny ourselves from giving or receiving it, we deny the very essence of that which we are made from. Nothing else can make us rise to the highest peaks or fall to the lowest valleys like love. Many moments are defined by the very presence of love. Love empowers you to touch the soul of your highest self and your divine nature. To stand before the universe with an open heart, in the face of fear and hurt, is the ultimate act of courage and freedom. Love is the energy in which were derived, and it is the destination that we continually seek. Our spirit was birthed and brought to life when the love energy was breathed into us. Love has the power to transcend circumstances, environments, hate, loneliness, and pain. When we allow ourselves to be open to it, we become truly alive. Life becomes more magical and more meaningful. Love prepares us for our ultimate destiny and releases our hearts from regret, resentment, and retribution. We will finally be able to reach our deepest depths compassion, empathy, kindness, courage, and generosity. Love is pure energy.

It can never be diminished or destroyed. Love is a divine energy that is always present and always flowing. If we can accept it, we realize that past hurts have nothing to do with love itself. We don't have to attempt to limit our love because we are a source of an unlimited supply. It is always generating. Feel its abundance inside of you and all around you. To become one with love is to become one with yourself.

BE STRONG ENOUGH

Be strong enough to let go of all the things that don't add value to your life. Be strong enough to walk away from toxic situations. Be strong enough to forgive without hearing an apology. Be strong enough to get up after being knocked down ninety-nine times. Be strong enough to say no. Be strong enough to trust yourself again. Be strong enough to be your own source of motivation. Be strong enough to ask for help. Be strong enough to cry when you're hurt. Be strong enough to admit when it's not okay. Be strong enough to be honest with yourself. Be strong enough to admit when you're wrong. Be strong enough to speak up. Be strong enough to stand for what's right. Be strong enough to love yourself in spite of. Be strong enough to forgive yourself. Be strong enough to have love for people who don't love you back. Be strong enough to give to others who have nothing to give you in return. Be strong enough to ask questions when you don't understand. Be strong enough to follow your heart. Be strong enough to be yourself.

HEART CLOSED FOR REPAIRS

The closing of a heart begins with hurt. We were born full of love, but pain caused it to leak from our lives. Maybe we weren't cared for the way we needed. People may have abandoned us when we needed them most. We could have been abused by the very people who we looked to for love. Maybe we didn't get the attention, we were bullied, or we were rejected. Thus, begins the process of building a wall around our hearts. After each undesirable experience we have, we add another layer to the wall, attempting to reinforce it until we deem it to be impenetrable. Even the chosen few we allow inside the wall only gets a piece of who we are. They are only allowed to see glimpses of what we truly have to give. Over time, the wall gets so thick that not only can love not get in, love can no longer get out. No matter how hard we may try, we cannot bind love. We cannot cage it like an animal we don't want to escape. We can't trap it in hopes of keeping as much as we can to ourselves. Love can't be limited to a certain space or environment. Love cannot be confined to the heart. In our attempt to protect love, we are only limiting it with fear. You can't own it or lose it. Love is not a delicate thing. Love is unequivocally the most powerful force and spirit in the universe. We are only hurting ourselves when we try to build a wall around us and around our hearts. We limit the fullness of what our lives were meant to be and cut ourselves off from the true power source. It's okay to be mindful of our hearts, and we should be careful with who we allow into our spiritual heart space. But don't close yourself off from the very thing you were meant to be the greatest source of.

IF YOU LET IT

Just because something is meant to happen doesn't mean that it was meant to be. Everything happens for a reason, but it may not happen for the reason we think. Trust your spirit, and let life unfold. It may not always work, but it will work out. If you let it.

DEAR SOUL

Dear Soul, I'm still learning. I'm still growing. And it's okay.

THE WOUNDS OF YESTERDAY

The surest route through pain and hurt is love. There will never be a moment when love has more potential to heal than in this moment. It is not lost. Love is ever-present. We must stop rekindling the flames on ancient hurts. Let the wounds of yesterday heal.

MOMENT OF CLARITY

When we open up the curtains of worry and doubt, we allow the bright light of breakthrough to shine on us and in us. It only takes a small ray of light to burn through the armor of pain and negativity around you. We can dig up in faith what we buried in fear. Life is no longer in black and white but is now able to display the full spectrum of vibrant colors. This energizes us and gives us access to our hidden divine powers to create and connect. We can connect to the world around us once more. We can look past the storm to see the sunshine. We can look past the pain and see love.

COLLECTIVE CONSCIOUSNESS

We live in a time unlike any the world has ever seen. The world has become a very noisy place. Potential is being wasted. Speed and convenience have become the language of the people. Truth has been mutated from a foundational state of being to a narrative created to serve one's own selfish endeavors. Too many of us are sacrificing big dreams for quick wins. Decency, integrity, and humility continue to be overshadowed by entitlement. The promised land evades us as people keep being delayed by those who are blinded by self-adoration, deafened by hate, and poisoned by ancient misguided ideals. The grind to greatness has been replaced by the comfort of mediocrity. The lack of human goodness has resulted in extreme levels of irresponsible behavior. There is no longer a clear line in the sand between right and wrong. Rare is it to find those with the courage to speak up or stand when their fellow man is dying and suffering. Generations are perishing without role models and without true leaders. Worldly comforts are numbing souls to the cries of pain around them. They are blind because they choose not to see. They are deaf because they choose not to hear. They share responsibility for the pain because they choose not to act. Our nations are plagued with unjustifiable poverty and unconscionable greed. If we continue on the path, our potential as a people will be wasted, and our true destiny will be cheated. We must strive to do better, and we must strive to be better. In each one of us lives a genuine place of love, humility, and peace, but we must have the courage to act on it. We must pick up those who have fallen. We must comfort those who have lost. We must be the strength for those who are in moments of weakness. We must make it our mission and responsibility to lift up those around us. It is the life purpose of each and every one of us to elevate humanity. To look through the temporary exterior and see the soul of the individual. To see beauty in all. To see love. To lead others to see and activate the potential in themselves and in their lives. We must strive to mend the divide and become a collective consciousness. We must awaken our power and lift the weight of the world from the backs of those struggling. We must consult our higher selves and choose to care about others and the world around us.

CHILDREN OF GREATNESS

If we can inspire ourselves, we can inspire the world. We are but a reflection of the individuals who share in our shared life experiences. We must choose to not accept less than when we are greater. We are approaching a new dawn of men and women of great character and substance. The mantle has been lifted from previous generations and has been placed solely at the feet of these children of greatness.

DON'T MISS THIS MOMENT

The aim of life is to live. It is not meant to just be, but to be vibrant, deeply felt, and meaningful. To be fully engaged and unconditional. To be lived in moments, not minutes. To be beautiful. To be fascinating. Life is meant to be celebrated. To be full of joy and blessings. There is so much more of life. Approach life with focus. Experience life with awareness. Feel life with depth. Digest life with meaning. If you can do that, you will shift chaos to order, chains to freedom, and storms to peace. Breathe. Feel. Sense your heart. Connect with your spirit. Don't miss the moment.

THE PAIN

Sometimes, you must hurt in order to know, fall in order to grow, and lose in order to gain because most of life's greatest lessons are learned through pain. Pain doesn't define you, but what you learn from it and what you do with it will determine the level that you will rise from it.

YOUR BIGGEST FAN

Sometimes, it may be hard for you to be consistent when no one is watching you, clapping for you, or pushing you. You have to clap for yourself. You have to push yourself. What you want to accomplish has to be important enough for you to want to do it for yourself. Be your biggest fan!

IN LOVE

Everything changes when you begin to fall in love with yourself. You will no longer send out the energy of desperation. No longer will you need to be filled from the outside. You become a powerful source within yourself that attracts bigger and better into your life. The more you love who you are, the less you seek validation and approval. Believe that!

BAGGAGE

We all have baggage to sort through. We decide what's coming into our lives by what we choose to unpack and leave behind. So many times, we carry so much with us in life that it holds us back and holds us down from rising to the place where we belong. We can allow ourselves to be prisoners of our past mistakes. We can let the opinions of others place limitations on our lives. We can carry the pain of old emotional wounds that have yet to heal. We can allow the fear of rejection to keep us from doing things we actually want to do. In order to be free of those things oppressing your present and your future, you have to unpack them from inside of you and leave them behind. That baggage is heavy and much more than you were meant to carry. So, forgive yourself and the past. Learn how to talk to yourself like someone who believes in you and knows the greatness you're capable of. Allow yourself to follow your spirit, get out of your comfort zone, and take risks. Give yourself permission to allow people who truly care to be there for you and support you. And most of all, be unapologetic about your truth and your story because it is the very thing that will help you become who you were meant to be.

BOUNDARIES

S et your boundaries, but still be open to change. It sounds simple, but for many of us, it becomes one or the other. We may set boundaries, but we become closed, closed-minded, and stubborn. We may be open to change, but that change has no definitive direction or purpose and leads to getting taken advantage of and taken for granted. You have to set your boundaries and your standards up front. That goes for anything (business, relationships, friendships). You have to set that expectation right from the beginning, and you confirm them by what you allow and how you allow others to treat you.

TRUE LEADERSHIP

True leadership is not about control, it's about service. True leadership is not about power, it's about empowering. It's not about manipulation, it's about inspiration. It's not about people, it's about purpose. True leadership is about becoming more than doing.

IN NOW

Don't run from this moment for yesterday or tomorrow. You can no longer allow yourself to be absent from this day or this moment. All that matters is that you choose to live now to the fullest of your truth. In now, is a possibility to be explored. In now, is an opportunity to be found. In now, is the fullness of a life to be lived.

ANTHONY D BRICE

AUTHOR'S FINAL THOUGHTS

One of the greatest gifts ever bestowed upon humanity is our power to choose. No matter who are, no matter where you're from and no matter what you've been through, you have the final say of who you will become. You have the final say of the kind of life that you want to create. It's not always going to be easy, it's not always going to be fair but how you show up in those moments will determine your future. This isn't a book that claims to have all of the answers. This isn't a book that claims to solve all of your problems. The purpose of this book is simply to be a mirror to help reveal you to your true self. A journey of self-discovery about how we learn to navigate through some of life's biggest personal challenges. Just like any other journey, this one will be a different experience for each and every person. That's the beauty of it. That's the power in it. The revelations and the epiphanies that you experience have nothing to do with anyone else and everything to do about you. My hope is that this book either reminded you or revealed to you, just how amazing you are. I hope that it showed you that everything that you're searching for is already living inside of you. As unbelievable and far-fetched as some of these statements may seem to some, I am reminded every day by the hundreds of people who reach out to me, just how powerful those words can actually be. If this book has helped you in any way, I hope that you are compelled to share the words with others who may need to hear them. I never realized just how impactful specific words in an exact moment could have on a person's life. It can change someone's day and it can ultimately change someone's life. I would like to sincerely thank all of you who sent me messages about how much a difference I've made in your life and that I should keep inspiring people. If it weren't for you, this book would have never been written. Thank you for taking this journey with me.

Anthony D Brice
email: soulrichbook@gmail.com
Instagram: @soulrichbook

CONTINUE THE JOURNEY

VISIT WWW.SOULRICHBOOK.COM